The adventures, misadventures, shames and triumphs,

THE SUBSTITUTE'S HANDBOOK:

A SURVIVOR'S GUIDE

The world's second oldest profession. . .revisited; a compendium of what to do, with whom, how frequently, where, why, when, and how, and other suggestions on ways to do it better for more enjoyment and greater satisfaction.

by
John Brenot

Published by
R & E Publishers
P. O. Box 2008
Saratoga, California 95070

Library of Congress Card Catalog Number
84-60972

I.S.B.N.
0-88247-729-3

Here are some figures that I'd like to call to your attention. They come from the 1983 *Statistical Abstract*. In 1980 (the latest figures available) for the fall semester there were 2,183,538 teachers; their average salary nationally was $16,780; there were 15,601 local school districts operating; secondary enrollment that year was 13,319,120 of which 1,000,000 would drop out during the school year; and for the year 1979-80 the average pupil expenditure was $2,494. Now if teachers take an average five days of sick leave for which they get paid and the 15,601 school districts have to pay substitute salaries over that, we're talking about a lot of money. At $25 per day that's $272,942,250 per year, nationwide for sub salaries. And that's *every* year. I know of a couple of school districts that aren't getting their money's worth.

To put that another way:
(Figures for 1980 are from the 1983 *Statistical Abstract*)
  15,601 local school districts nationwide
  2,183,538 teachers nationwide
  $16,780 average teacher's salary nationwide
If: 2,183,538 teachers take an average of 5 substitute days per year and if a sub on the nationwide average is paid $25 per day:
  2,183,538 x 5 x $25 = $272,942,250 per year (and that's *every year*) paid for substitute salaries nationwide.

Note
  13,319,120 students are enrolled
  1,000,000 students drop out each year (7.5% drop out)
  $2,494 spent per student per year
1,000,000 x $2,494 = $2,494,000,000 wasted each year nationwide on students who drop out of school before their education is completed. Nationally we are doing something wrong. These figures represent a huge waste of both money and human re-

sources and potential.

As Everett Dirksen once said, "A million here and a million there and pretty soon you're talking about real money." You're also talking about real people, too.

Apologia: *Many teachers, parents or subs don't understand the sorts of language that have become commonplace for many students these days, so be forewarned. The terms that may shock you a bit are direct quotations from students.*

Series are punctuated the old-fashioned way for clarity. If you say math, science, French and English history, that's quite a different message from math, science, French, and English history. If it isn't clear, it's wrong.

There must be some other reason substitutes do it. It certainly can't be the money; multiply $40 times every possible school day of the year (40 x 180 days) and the grand total is a cool $7,200. If you have a family, you qualify for welfare. The custodial staff and groundsmen make a lot more money than you can, but of course the paradox here is that you're considered overly qualified to do such menial tasks.

It can't be the satisfactions gained from an administration that seems unaware of how to smooth out some potentially disastrous days for everyone involved when a substitute is on campus. The basic and essential aids are so simple.

It can't be the kind, generous, and gracious greetings you often get from the existing faculty. How often does anyone even bother to rephrase the "Who are you, today?" standard? You're no one but the interloper who has temporarily replaced someone who has as much purpose, legitimacy, stature, and expertise as the one who is asking you who you are. Which do you prefer? To whom it may concern, or Dear Occupant? This really struck home one morning when I arrived at a school whose machinery had broken down, and I wasn't needed that day after all. When asked, "Who are you, today?" without hesitation, I answered, "I'm nobody today." That was a really eerie feeling. Visiting the office on a day when I didn't work at that school, when asked who I was, the reply came out, "I'm myself today." That felt better.

It certainly isn't the warmth and understanding you get from those eager little pupils, ready with pens poised to copy down every nuance of what you are saying. No, siree. That's rare enough for the regular teacher, but we're talking now about substitutes.

It has got to be something else rather obviously. It's got to be the interesting challenge presented.

After the first few hours, I thought that maybe I had burned out on substituting and ought to consider seriously some alternative professional goal at which I could excel, hold my own, or at least survive. But, alas, that has not been my lot and that is also why it became imperative that I analyze what was happening, with whom, how many times, and then what I could do about it. And that was the challenge. And that's why I'm writing this; not to unveil the mysteries of the secret oriental elixir which will allow you to know it all theoretically, but to offer simple and practical instructions to substitutes on how to make it happen better, hour after hour, and day by day.

When the substitute folder came through the mail I was startled as I hadn't expected that sort of thing. When I opened it I was even more so, because on the first page and on its own reverse an identical message of welcome-to-the-club from the superintendent was printed. The next page listed the various members of the board of education, the superintendent's "cabinet" and staff. The reverse of that page was blank. The following page was grandly titled the Table of Contents: the reverse of that was blank also. For seven pages then there was

3

some general information of expectations, hours of "service," classroom control; etc. Armed with all of that knowledge plus a few additional pages of data like district holidays; oh boy, days you either don't get to or have to work, depending on how things are going, I still didn't know very much.

If that had been the sum total of my expertise in being a substitute for them, I wasn't going to be very effective; and I wasn't. At first it was all quite mysterious, but gradually, after some really good experiences and some equally disastrous ones, I began to see that there were some interesting patterns forming. I went home each afternoon and began making voluminous notes on what had happened right and wrong, how to correct deficiencies, how to approach the exact same lesson and make it work better. I took a lot of chances with other people's classes and by trying one technique for a class hour and trying something quite different the next, I was able to see that certain lesson formats were better than others, that the character of the regular instructor affected the atmosphere of the classroom even when not there, that a presumed control or lack of it made all sorts of difference in how it all went.

Remember that irrelevant educational psychology class you took even before you started teaching (the B. F. Skinner behavior modification stuff), all of that drivel about wire and cloth mothers, negative and positive reinforcement? We were going to be dealing with children, not pigeons and monkeys. Children were more sophisticated than that; they were rational animals. Such primitive techniques would never work. Alas!

A junior high low-end boy in a special reading class farted on cue (that was "passed wind" when I was a boy) every time the teacher was trying to make a major point about something. In tears finally, she went to the principal and also asked her colleagues at the lunchtable what to do. One teacher said, "I couldn't help but laugh;" another said, "He should be removed from class?" another said, "Ignore it; and it'll go away by itself." Which you would do would affect that class enormously. That kind of behavior would continue until it was no longer rewarded in any way.

When I was a kid it was de rigueur for students to at least try to put-on a substitute. It was the thing to do. Little in that direction has changed. I began to notice that I could

4

affect student perception through body language, though. It was fun to try different techniques here too, and I found that there is only a minor variation from a low to an accelerated group. They all want to feel warm and comfortable.

When I was still a teacher, I was interested primarily in curriculum development. I burned-out when I stopped doing that and relied entirely on old lessons. I had never consciously thought about classroom management and to have to review the physical act of teaching and concentrate on the way you moved, said certain things, and manipulated behaviors by doing this or that was very foreign to my make-up. I must have been doing something right instinctively all those years, because I felt that I had good relationships with students. I know I spent a lot of time reviewing what had gone wrong after that first miserable year of teaching.

I realized, too, that the solutions to so many years of student negative conditioning against sub days would be possible only when education was viewed as a cooperative venture among the various categories of people in a school.

Then I decided to write my own version of a substitute's handbook, and here it is:

To the Substitute:

Before any class starts, print your last name in block letters in the upper left or right outside corner of the blackboard with the date directly below. Make the letters large and plain; it adds power. Do put Miss or Mrs. (Ms. will challenge some types of students) there. Don't put Mr. Students won't transgress that boundary, I've found, until they feel so comfortable around you that they may call you Dude or Bro by mistake. It's a compliment actually, not an insult. You're okay. You can easily tell if they're being rude or unruly.

The Cattle Drive and the Roundup:
Those five minutes before classes are crucial ones for you. This is the time for you to take your positioning (body language). I had played with a variety of places to stand or slump before I came onto the place which seems to work best. At the spot where the classroom is already focused by

the teacher: the teacher's desk or lectern usually, lean back on the desk with your rear resting against the edge or stand leaning to one side of the lectern. I call this my jellyfish. I am the most non-threatening authority figure you ever saw.

As each kid comes into the classroom try to get direct eye contact, smile, and wish them, "Good morning". They will frankly be disoriented because no sub ever pulled this routine before; isn't this turkey aware of what's just minutes away? But there's some kind of cumulative effect, and it works. You stiffen, even slightly, only when someone comes on with some behavior that you can't ignore.

Try to avoid any isolation between you and the class. Be out there and among them, not up there hidden away behind any kind of protective barrier. Don't even fold your arms; you must be totally open.

During the progress of the day you will have to amend your jellyfish configuration (it's the Dali Clock Syndrome), especially if low groups misperceive your calmness for weakness. Spring into action if you need to, but return as soon as possible to the most sag you can get away with. Try to add or subtract a few layers of physical threat at a time, rather than one by one.

Most crucial times of the day are obviously before and after nutrition break, an assembly, and especially before and after lunch and just before the end of school.

Hold the seating chart in your hand for quick reference. Scan that group like a hawk for any signs of anti-social behavior. This is your first assessment time. The movements, noise level, general activity will give you interesting clues on how to deal with that particular group. Each class seems to develop a singular personality. Often the kid who declares open season when he sees the sub, is not the one who is your nemesis. You're safer with body language here. Give the verbal one a broader smile, a laugh, some extra eye contact and you've usually made a friend. You must find out the names of any students who threaten you in the least. They are the key to control that hour.

The Roundup:
You're going to have some milling around, so you say the most obvious thing that's possible: "Please be in your seat (not seats. Seats is more than one. You want to separate

6

and isolate each class member.) when the bell rings." If you slip up on the time you can still say safely, "The bell has rung. please take your seat." Get up and close the door. You don't need any other distractions or random diversions. Keep the class as isolated as possible. Don't move too rapidly; walk away more rapidly than you come back.

Roll:

If there's an accurate and up-to-the-minute seating chart. read each name and gain eye contact with each student in turn. If you use the alphabetical roll sheet, have each student answer "Here" and raise his hand. That seems to act as a settling-in exercise as they are now no longer anonymous. Each student seems to feel more personally responsible; you have penetrated some sort of armor by knowing who he is. Make sure you know the names of any hardcore wiseacres and don't hesitate to use them. They will be startled when you do, because no one has ever bothered to learn them before, apparently. But those are the key students for class control in a strange school. Do a poll or anything else you can think of to get students to identify themselves.

If you have only the attendance roll sheets as the teacher has all others with him, don't let them be taken away by the attendance people. If you can, xerox an additional copy for you; if you can't, keep them and be one class hour behind in attendance reporting. You must not lose a way to identify students.

Even with the most up-to-date seating chart on your side. there is a tendency toward musical chairs when students see a substitute. Trade-offs so that they may sit near a friend are pretty common. When you call roll. apologize for mispronouncing names. (Kids are very sensitive about this and appreciate your concern for some reason.)

After roll, replay the names of the people you have marked absent. "Are there any others I've missed?" Few kids want to be counted absent when they're not: and if there have been musical names, you'll know that then. Time for a poll if you feel that it is necessary.

Don't introduce yourself. I had been told to do that; but don't. I tried a sixty-second rap on who I was and why, until one rude child said, "What does that have to do with English?" He was right and I was wasting their time: they didn't care who I was. Get on with the lesson; that's why these students came to school today. If you return to the same school frequently, gradually they'll ask you or you will reveal some things about yourself without thinking about it. Don't rush anything.

One major question frequently asked of male subs is whether he is gay. Answer that one immediately. Even though you're really adept at delivering biting sarcasm, don't say, "Is there some special reason you want to know?" The rest will probably laugh, but that embarrasses the kid who asked, and you've made at least one enemy. Even if the question doesn't come up, I've noticed in classes that if early on I make some allusion to my teenage sons or my wife, there's a general relaxing of tension. You can see students slump slightly. They're very insecure about this issue, so it seems better to face it frontally. If I were a devisive bachelor, I'd be tempted to invent a wife. My wife, who is teaching somewhere else, is doing so and so, is a, has three, believes in, enjoys the game of, who is also a blond, loves to garden, whose favorite color is, plays tennis well, etc. She exists, sort of.

When students ask what's wrong with the regular teacher, if you don't know, make something up. Don't get scandalous with lurid tales of back alleys and smoky dens and loose women. But also don't say you don't know. They want a valid reason for a member of their family not to be there. The reason for this is that often you're subbing out of your own field. If you don't know very much about the subject of that class, you don't know how to pronounce students' names, you don't even know what's wrong with the teacher, you must be a pretty stupid person. It's better to know something about why the teacher's not there at least. Keep it simple; a dental problem, a field trip, a conference or workshop are always acceptable. You can elaborate a little and put in a little humor; and they'll feel comfortable about that; and you were the bearer of the information that they wanted to have right then. It's necessary for us to improvise and carry on, if the reason chosen was an emergency and

8

comedy of errors; if you choose this one you will imply that we must cooperate together to continue with a stiff upper lip the important things being done in class. It's a good technique, especially for upper range students.

Never be the bearer of bad tidings. The person who says it openly is held responsible for the fact that it exists and is resented. Let the regular teacher tell them the truth if that is his style. Be sure to note which reason you gave on your capsule of the day sheet.

Don't ever say that the teacher is having an R and R. Students will feel abandoned and not want to be there either. The class will be more restless and you won't have made the teacher's lot any easier either.

Tell them if you know when the teacher will come back. If it's tomorrow that's fine, and today becomes less threatening; if it's three days from now you gain control power.

As part of the class assessment phase I also began to ask the class a question that was really relevant to me. "When you see a substitute what is your reaction? How do you feel?" When I got replies back like, "It's nice to have a different face sometimes;" or "You looked like a nice person I thought I might like," I knew I had a very reasonable group for that hour. On the other hand if the bulk of the replies were, "Another sub who can't keep control", or "We're going to have some fun this hour," my task was to be more like ringmaster.

I've got freaky hair. I devised a simple test: Do I look more like Gene Wilder (a nice association with *Charlie and the Chocolate Factory*) or the late comedian Marty Feldman (*Young Frankenstein*)? If I got a lot of Gene Wilder's, I had a better group that hour than a lot of Marty Feldman's. The opening atmosphere began to change dramatically. The more relaxed I looked the more frequently I was getting non-hostile replies to my reaction to a substitute question.

The two boys walked through the door. They were tall and athletic, nice looking kids. One of them said, "Oh boy, a substitute" with such joy that my heart fell to the floor. The other did a little jig and vaguely swaggered to his seat. I was in for it and I didn't know what to do. I scrambled through

An anonymous student work in response to the question:
"How do you feel when you have a substitute?"

the materials left for me to find the seating chart; there wasn't one. No help there. (I thought that at least the first instinct of a student was usually to home-in on his own seat before any later shifting might be done.) I'd wait for roll then and note my adversaries. We then played the little game of musical names. I'll be Mark and you be Sean. The class was a disaster. I had no power to do anything about an impossible situation. As a friend said, "You're there, and you're all alone."

That night I resolved to recommend that all teachers be required to leave accurate and up-to-the-minute seating charts. That would help some.

Corralled:

But the real problem was that I had no way of verifying who was who or said he was. And then it struck me that I could do that by giving each student a sheet of the school district's paper.

Polls. Here is a device for getting the information you need: namely, that kid's name. It's called the poll. I explained that I was taking a course at a nearby university, was gathering field data for a presentation necessary for my advanced degree. Would they help me? You bet! Let's set the record straight, man. The topic was: What are today's teen-agers *really* like?

Now don't get involved in loaded questions like: Should the homecoming princesses be reimbursed for their dresses; yes, no, and why?" or "It has been suggested that your school colors be changed. What colors would you like and why?" The place will crumble before your very eyes.

Instead, stick to some nice, safe areas. Stretch it out with: What kinds of cars most appeal to today's teenagers, body design, color, number or doors, etc? In other words, some questions which deal with what is uppermost in their minds like sex, and drugs, and rock and roll.

To avoid a future academic challenge (by a jealous and covetous colleague, of course) they need to put in the upper right hand corner of their paper: their name, the name of their school, and the date. Give the first question and begin to circulate. Ask them a maximum of five questions. They'll lose interest after that, and that's enough time to circulate more than once around. Circulate first on the side of the room away from the troublemakers. If they feel attacked and vulnerable, they'll put their hands over their names and you will have accomplished nothing.

Another possible addition to the poll: the assertiveness question. You've been waiting in the supermarket line for twenty minutes. It's the day before a major holiday; everyone has been buying huge baskets full of foods; everyone is busy and behind schedule and perhaps irritable. A large well-built (expensively dressed or whatever you like, elaborate at will but make the guy self-assured to the point of boorishness) man cuts directly in front of you. What would you do? On a scale from "fall him out for knuckle drill" (aggressive) to "I wouldn't do anything" (a total squish), you can determine as you circulate what the temper of the majority of the group is. Reduce the answers to: Knuckle drill, Speak to, Call the manager, Say nothing, so that it can be read easily. Also ask this as question number one so that it will be on the top of the paper.

Some additional possibilities:

1. Which musical group has been the most influential and why? (Don't ask this question in a junior high or a low-end high school class; they'll start singing.)

2. If you had complete freedom to choose, how would you change your image?

3. If you had an ideal substitute day, what would that be like?

4. Would you learn more or less about the primary topics or subjects of this class with your teacher or sub here and why? (You'd be amazed at how many kids think their regular teachers know very little.)

5. How would you describe the VP? (Expect some raspberries and don't actually do this one; it was our little joke. The whole class will come apart.)

6. Name your future livelihood. Why did you choose that particular occupational area?

12

The possibilities are endless and do notice that not one question has dealt with the declared purpose of the poll. No one has ever seemed to notice.

If you're getting strange feedback and inconsistent body language during the Roundup Period, try this technique as an opener. It's freely adopted from the *Six to Eight Stages of Moral Development*.

Your mate is dying of cancer. She needs a rare and costly drug to stay alive while new cures are being developed. You are unemployed and broke. What would you do? (Have them write.) Ask each student to justify his action. Ask, "How many of you are concerned with being punished by your father-in-law or God if you don't help?" You've skipped the conjugal pleasure number one moral level, and have asked number two instead. Go through the other stages and later ask if there are any other reasons for your action? You may then get some level ones.

Don't be judgmental; and don't explain the system to the students. You want to know where the majority of this group is coming from so that you can gear the hour accordingly. Use this for upper classmen only. Whatever question is used must be appropriate to the age level of the students being asked.

Use the poll sparingly. It's not going to take very long, if every sub who walks into class is taking a course at the nearby university and in order to satisfy the requirements for an advanced degree. . .for those students to smell a rat. Treat this as a desperation move. But do vary the diet and come on with some significant variations if you do use it.

Another technique. Hand a sheet of paper down each row and have each kid sign in. Let them know that that will account for their being in class that day (and you have a ready-made, makeshift seating chart to use). The hazard here is a reprise of musical names. How many Bob Marley's, Dick Whittington's and Bill Cosby's are enrolled in American high schools? I don't know why these names have become so popular. If I ever run into a real one, I know I won't be able to believe it.

If the classroom teacher will help you with reliable seating charts and roll sheets, this kind of chicanery may become unnecessary and obsolete. Just in case, carry a ream of foolscap with you each day. Don't cut it into small pieces. Students perceive half-sheets with less seriousness than whole ones and tend to write smaller. Remember, you're there to get names, not information. Don't buy that paper yourself; let the district pay. If you find the atmosphere of any particular class hour non-threatening, don't use the poll at all. Use it only when you feel you absolutely have to. Don't ever throw these away at school; they must be taken home and burned.

Or, if you have time devise some sort of test. "Put your name on the paper and number from one to ten" usually strikes terror in the hearts of the most immune types. Circulate while you give them the "test".

With a class that comes in on a roar after an assembly, it may be worth the waste of thirty-five sheets of paper. If the teacher has done it for you by sending the right kind of lesson, don't use the poll; it's redundant. It will take a little time and more threatening stances from you to calm them down is all.

There are roughly one hundred and fifty to two hundred and fifty students during a day and only one of you. No matter how sharp you may feel, there's got to be one among them who is way ahead of you. He may have less to concentrate on than you; he may have a flash of inspiration; he may become aware of deja vu. Deny any manipulation.

"Haven't we done this assignment before? It looks familiar." (a student)

"Why, every day you're here, do we have written-out assignments?" (a student)

"It's easy for you, but what of all these other subs? Detention will be overflowing." (a VP)

"Are all administrators ex-teachers who have risen to their level of incompetency?" (a teacher)

"Do you remember how you were taught to remember the difference between principle and principal? He's your pal." (a teacher)

The VP and a teacher at that same school, who was a member of the opposite sex, were living openly together in the same dwelling place. The teacher was transferred to a different school within the district. Their crime wasn't defined, but there were a lot of innuendos. Pressure had been applied by the ladies of the PTA, and the district administration had crumbled in the face of the righteousness of their moral crusade.

There must have been some sort of assumption on the part of the ladies that there was a lot of spare time for teachers and administrators during the school day, and those twenty minutes before and after, to indulge themselves and each other in some sort of goings on. As I recollect, probably the last thing on anyone's mind during the school day is sex.

To the Administration:

One of the basic goals of the administration has seemed to be keeping the lid on things so that it will go along pretty much as usual; e.g., to actively seek peace and quiet.

Each member of the team is going to have to bestir himself, however, add a little extra pressure at the beginning, and do what's necessary to begin to solve the sub problem. It's been runaway for as long as I can remember, and it's not necessary to keep feeding it with inaction.

The solutions seem to be a great deal simpler than anyone dreamed. And once the process begins it will tend to radiate out and have cumulative effect.

The administration must prepare a substitute folder which contains:

1.   a map of the school (with faculty restrooms, lounge, lunchroom noted in one color) (departmental offices, library, AV, Xerox room, etc..

15

noted differently).

2. a bell schedule — writ large. "May we go early?" "No, I *know* what time we're supposed to leave."

3. a listing of some *unique* rules of the school if there are any.

4. pads of various attendance, hall pass forms, detention slips.

5. a listing of the standardized attendance symbols.

6. a brief explanation of attendance procedures and when the master attendance is to be done for the day.

7. a copy of the master schedule or the regular teacher's schedule.

Don't let the secretaries fuddle around getting keys in between phone calls. This is precious time for the substitute that's often wasted. At one school the receptionist clips keys on the folder, and it's totally self-contained when you get there. She also tells you where the office coffee pot is and offers to get some for you. It's a nice hospitable touch.

The administration must be willing to give the substitute power. Don't ask a substitute to note people who have destroyed a reasonable class atmosphere. He shouldn't have to convince the regular teacher of the necessity for punishing the wrong-doer. That's analogous to the mother who tells her child that he will be punished when the father gets home later that night. She loses her credibility as a force to be reckoned with, and her power is her husband. The last thing a sub needs is a student perception of him as a passive female type. Power can be a graded paper or project, detention, a holding tank for expelees from class, some levers for the slow learner to be made aware that you mean business.

Incidentally, for the homecoming father-teacher, who just wanted his children to love and respect him, now he has been unwillingly cast in the role of punisher and someone to be feared, not trusted. Everyone loses in this scenario.

The administration might consider:

1. The character and quality of sub's lessons as an aspect of a teacher's evaluation. If only certain types of lessons really work to advantage for a substitute, why not require more of that style of format?

2. The sub knows instantly whether:
   a) the lesson is a valid one that continues the flow of information in the class,

   b) is a nice diversion for the students that day from the regular "work",

   c) is just plain B.S.

3. The sub might be asked to evaluate the ease with which he could get the class going, too.

The administration might reconsider the character of some of their hirees. If the school atmosphere is to be a pleasant one where the kid wants to be, sub selection practices need to be reviewed. Quotation from a student's journal: "Well, we got a substitute a little while ago for Mr. Stone and I can't believe but he's a tall, lame faggot. He paints his fingernails red and orange and he says it makes him look better. His name is Mr. Marsh. Everyone calls him a fag and he just says, "What's wrong with that?" We like to ask him lots of questions. . .he doesn't answer. When he came to sub for us he wore these real loose shorts with a hole in them so you could see. Gross me out. When he throws a football, he looks like a gay. I hope we never have him again but others do like him, if you know what I mean. Well, the new guy Jim got along with him real well. . ."

The administration might consider some other means of sub selection. Perhaps some people ought not be on anyone's campus; they're just not right as substitutes. Perhaps a test could be devised that could accurately measure a candidate's profile and levels of the following negative and positive qualitites listed by students. Someone who

1. is vague and remote, not positive, is dumb, and doesn't know anything;

2. is fearful and tentative; doesn't trust or like students;

3. doesn't demand quiet, order, and doesn't assume control;

4. isn't gentle; threatens students by speech and posture;

5. isn't perceived as a nice person or an interesting one;

6. has some real weakness, is gay, a "jerk", has phobias, is perceived as socially inferior to the students;

7. is erratic and unstable himself; is perceived as "unfair" and is inconsistent in dealing with a variety of situations;

8. is perceived as being patronizing and/or "stuck up".

However, someone who:

1. maintains an adult distance, is not too familiar;

2. is comfortable to be with, kind of like a favorite aunt or uncle who looks out for others;

3. can be firm, expects performance, but is warm —

that person has the personal qualities needed to be a successful substitute.

Sorry about the disproportion on the negative side but those are the results I got. A test like this might also be used in teacher training programs for potential candidates who could be retrained if they exhibited too many negative and not enough positive characteristics.

Hands up for volunteers! Has any administrator considered offering the opportunity to his staff of organizing a substitute exchange program? The English teacher from one school would take the classes of the chemistry teacher from an entirely different district. The day could be structured: one class would have accurate seating charts and roll sheets; another would have only one or the other. The lessons during the day could be quite varied, too: lecture one hour, group activities for another, perhaps a dittoed lesson for contrast. It could be quite an enlightening and interesting experience for your staff to reconsider who they are today.

"Mrs. Ellison (the library aide) has just come on with another commandment. This one is, 'Thou shall not socialize' (in the library)." Since the library is often the haven for the upper range and more timid students, why can't the library be divided into two sections: one for discussion and one for quiet. Glass partitions and a two-way speaker for monitoring noise levels can't be all that expensive. Don't furnish it with sofas and magazine racks as that will attract the campus loungers. They'll destroy the atmosphere for the others and perhaps demolish the facility itself. Keep it sparse; this is for an academic group. Perhaps the PTA ladies could be encouraged to organize an activity that would raise the funds for the partition. And that could be fun, too.

Unfortunately, the librarian is most frequently described by students as a "bitch" ; her image is so negative. The gentle, calm, quite intelligent, refined and very motherly type is the exception, and then the kids really like her. Her image could improve perceptibly if she weren't reduced to requiring absolute quiet all the time. Something as simple as a partition might be an answer.

I'm the first member of the Save The Holiday League and I wish you would join me. I would like to stop the subversive elements among us that have ruined, potentially at least, one of the nice unifiers of our culture, Halloween. If that seems frivolous and not terribly important, I wish that you would reconsider. In total the types of foods we tend to eat, the games we tend to play with one another, the holidays we share and anticipate as nice accent points along the way of our year, help make us who we are as a nation and we need to keep our national uniqueness as much intact as is possible.

We can't very well outlaw apples and razor blades (that's about as effective as outlawing guns), but we can adjust to a new reality. There are some really sick people out there in fantasyland. And they're willing to maim and murder children.

In order to protect them we're going to have to supervise and watch out more carefully for one another's children. When we lived in Cairo, American children were given a map of Anglo houses for trick and treating. We took them and some classmates around in the car. The Egyptians weren't trying to poison or mutilate them, they just don't celebrate Halloweeen and might think it a trifle odd if a hoard of little kids in weird costumes came begging at their doors in the nighttime. It's cumbersome but safer. If parents would organize smaller private parties, or better yet, the PTA ladies could do something useful and organize and supervise a fun-night carnival at school where security can be monitored more easily, that could help to reduce a dangerous situation. That would also make school the center for another pleasant activity.

A much neglected administrative function that could fill another real void, would be another social one. That too may sound trivial, but it's important. Some of the members of the all too typical teaching staff in schools I've visited are desperately lonely people. They work with kids all day and are tired at the end of a day. They've had enough of teenagers and need some mental stimulation or some diversion or some shared activity with someone over the age of eighteen.

If they live in the same community as the one where they teach, they rarely have a sense of real privacy. Each time that they buy a bottle of gin or a box of Kotex at the market and have to endure another knowing smile from the boxboy, there's a tendency to withdraw more and more. It's a vicious circle. You become even more protective of the little bit of privacy you do have and consequently isolate yourself.

One teacher told us that she was invited to a colleague's house for dinner for the first time after she had

20

taught in the same school for eight years. And that was the first time she had ever been in a fellow faculty member's house at all.

Brenot's Inflexible Law Of At Whose Convenience: In a school, anything that needs to be done will be accomplished at the convenience of the bus schedule, the bell schedule, the master schedule, the final exam or testing schedules, the athletic schedule, the activity schedule, the janitor, or the administration.

A retired teacher, when asked why she didn't supplement her income by substituting said, "I just can't do discipline all day."

"We had one sub with such terrible control that by the end of the hour, every kid in class had been sent to the office. Of course, only about half of them ever got there." (a teacher)

Overheard in the lunchroom, "Who is that guy?" "He's only a substitute."

To The Substitute:

There are a lot of ways for you to get a class quiet initially:

Be firm and really demand quiet vocally, facially, and by stance; say, "Quiet, please", "Let's begin", "Let's get started", "Let's take roll now."

Hold up a hand. Say and with a gesture, "Zip the lip."

Bellow, "Quiet".

Sit against a table or desk and wait.

Stand and glance at the clock (this is only useful if the clocks are on the side walls. If the clock is behind you, forget it; if it's behind the students it won't have an effect) or glance at your own watch and don't make this subtle.

"Quiet now!" and obviously count the time it takes to get the class quiet by holding up your watch. This is especially effective for classes before nutrition, lunch, and the end of school. You hold them for as long after the passing bell rings as it took to get them quiet. This can be effective for a regular teacher, long-term sub, or a frequent, well-known sub.

If you penalized a whole class yesterday, and the following day there are only a couple of holdouts, assign them detention or hold only them after class. The other members of the class will appreciate your being willing to differentiate and will apply pressures on the holdouts, themselves.

When you tack time on the end of a class, wait until it's absolutely quiet before you count the make-up time. But then tell them about something you feel would interest them and make the contact a pleasant one; you become really human after all.

For low range groups you must be much more forceful initially. They must realize that you are a presence. Once quiet is established, however, relax with them; they, too, will feel much more comfortable. Only stiffen when you need to quash some unacceptable behavior. You're better off being "cool" than a martinet.

Start talking, raise your volume slightly, then reduce it until you can talk normally. You may need to recap the first couple of sentences.

Do a pantomime in which you stitch your own mouth closed with an imaginary needle and thread. Usually by the time you get to the needle through the lips segment, they're ready to cooperate.

Usually some girl will say, "Come on, you guys!" Put

up a hand; do or say something right then; reinforce her remark with some action on your part. Begin with whatever you want, but preferably roll call. Get it out of the way and gain eye contact. Unmask them early.

There are a lot of ways to gain guiet; many more than these, but you've got to gain control through quiet. You can't teach anything unless it's quiet. Do note that quiet is a relative thing. Your classroom must not always be quiet. You must talk with students and they must have some space for verbal exploration and interchange. What you must always have under your contol is the ability to get them quiet at your option. Don't ever say, "Shut up" to students low, high, or medium either. They hate the phrase and think that it's really quite unacceptable. They feel that an adult who would use it is out of control himself.

After the lesson has begun, stand at the front of the classroom for a minute or two or until the last head has dropped toward the desk. Then start circulating slowly. Incidentally, I found that if I wanted the group to be really down, all I had to do was take the same route each time. I caused some agitation if I varied it. If that happens they are immediately reassured again if you make eye contact and smile.

Circulate with the roll sheet or seating chart with you. If you get just a fraction of a name you can usually put it together with some hints.

For any talkative holdouts or to reduce a last whis- pered conversation, begin to do something yourself (not read a magazine or newspaper; that's fatal) but begin to write and periodically glance at the students. It's somehow soothing or intimidating. And they tend not to want to dis- turb something important that you're doing. Writing is active, not passive. I have had students apologize for inter- rupting my writing, often while I was making notes for this handbook.

Don't *always* circulate. When the atmosphere calls for it, sit down. There must be some totally passive phases without movement or action for contact/contrast to be appreciated. There must be a time for absolute quiet that no one wants to shatter.

Don't always sit if the atmosphere is mellow, stand if

it's intermediate, or walk around if it's agitated. You can affect real changes if you're calmer-seeming than the mood would imply.

Never sit behind a desk. You're low and unimposing. Better is a tall stool out in the open and not behind a lectern. Better is to lean against the front of the desk, or turn a student chair around and sit on the writing tablet. Better is to circulate slowly in the room, obviously spending more time near any potential trouble spots or pockets of resistance.

On the other hand there's an enormous difference between circulating and stalking. Don't make students nervous with your movements. At times it's better to pause and sit down, especially as you sense a calming in the atmosphere.

In really upper range classes you'll probably want to circulate only once early in the class hour and somewhere between one-half to three-quarters of the way through, when there is a ripple of restlessness from monotony and boredom. You may want to tolerate for a brief period some quiet talking and calculator borrowings as they need to do something different. They work together effectively and enjoy helping one another, bouncing ideas back and forth. When they're totally with their own, they relax and enjoy the mental contests they never exhibit in a mixed grouping.

Only get authoritarian if the conversation drags on or expands to group size. Glance first, then say, "Shh", then move toward any persistent talkers. This kind of group has been conditioned to have enough self-discipline to get something accomplished during a class hour. They hate wasting time. You must establish early an easy rapport. They can be runaway if you misread them. They can be so calm that you think you must have hypnotized them into submission, too.

For low-enders note. To circulate may mean that you spend an inordinate amount of time in one area of the classroom over another also. Never hesitate to lean against the back wall. No regular teacher with any ego left intact will ever do this (they often don't particularly trust their students) so this is an interesting control stance and a new approach for them. It tends to make them uneasy in an easily controlled kind of way. If you feel any lessening of contact while you're in the back, move rapidly to the front and take any stance necessary to regain control.

Don't ever allow so much noise that another student can say that he can't concentrate on what he's doing as a result of the noise.

If you need to get a large group quiet, don't circulate too early. They need to know that you're there and if they can't see you then you lose your authority status. If the rumblings continue and you have talked quietly to several people individually, choose one obviously bright, upper-class, personally secure girl and from across the room in a genuine teacher voice say, "Allison, quiet!" Choose someone who never gets reprimanded for anything. The rest of the class will love it and think that justice has at last been done, by you, an impartial observer. It's an opening for them to be glad that you're there.

Don't use terms like, "Silence!" It's too old-fashioned and formal. Don't turn off any portion of your audience with an unnecessary red flag. Keep it simpler. Students would like the world to focus and refocus on their own time. It's what is important to them. They don't want a lot of harking back to the good old days stuff.

"Keep the noise down, please!" "It's too noisy now; you'll have to keep it down!" "You'll have to keep the noise to a minimum roar." These phrases seem to imply at least that you're still in control and are allowing some noise, nevertheless.

If you say the obvious for some reason it works. "Now listen carefully" when you really want to get something across; et voila; they actually do. Didn't you want them to listen equally intently all class hour? Realistically, you know better than that. And that's another reason for needing to vary lesson styles and create variety, breaks in the flow, accent marks during the classhour.

"I learned U. S. History only when I had to teach about it." (a teacher)

"I've got to teach penmanship." "You'd better teach them how to type instead." (one teacher to another)

Why are so many lessons for subs so poor? Have you ever called a sub to thank him for a job well done? Would you want your sister to marry one?

To the Teacher:

It's incredibly disheartening, after you're aware of what is necessary for a successful day, to find that all the cards are stacked against you. That's another reason that this handbook seemed to be so necessary as a device for re-educating teachers, too. The sooner students are required to view sub days more as business-as-usual rather than open-season, the sooner many of these problems described will have remedied themselves. Working together is the only way that can be accomplished.

Imagine a teacher who returns to school to choruses, whole roomsful of adoring disciples, who hears for several hours that day, "We're so glad you're back; that sub was horrible." That's a pretty effective conditioning process, isn't it?

What would happen if the regular teacher came back to school and the students *groaned*, or the students said that the sub was *better*, or the sub was more interesting, younger and prettier, *less* boring, or how about: even *more* boring; etc.?

How many students have put it together that the terrible lesson they're having that day was sent by their regular teacher? Is it a subconscious way of rejecting the family, even temporarily? The sub is the one up front who takes the rap for a bad lesson, however. (**To the Substitute:** Announce, "This is the lesson your teacher would like to have us work on this hour." If it's impossible; amend it. It's your survival.) Teachers need to do everything possible to reduce sub anxiety, not increase it.

Remember that we have a maximum of thirty minutes

26

after we arrive in a totally strange environment to find the main office, get our assignments, find your classroom, read the instructions of your lesson, get out any special equipment, texts, workbooks, colored chalk, and typically a lot of other stuff.

Please, have all materials in one place. There isn't time to go from your classroom to the Xerox room (whereever that is?), call the AV coordinator, get the booklet from the librarian, back to your office (whereever that is?), locate the locked cupboard, top shelf, right side where you've left something or other, and still have time to get an attitude on how to proceed for the day.

If there are needed materials call them by their correct titles and put them where you say they will be. You must remember the titles of those texts by now? Have chalk, pens, pencils, paper, stapler, etc., where we can find them. Preferably right next to the other needed things.

In case of a real emergency day, why not consider xeroxing duplicates of your class roll sheets and/or seating charts and attaching those to the emergency lesson plan? Learning names for the sub is his lifeline.

If you know in advance that you're going to be absent from school, tell your classes and prepare them for a substitute day. Tell them what the general assignment will be, that you expect their cooperation with the sub, and that you'd prefer being proud rather than ashamed of them. It's a little like instructions given to little kids before a friend's birthday party; thank the hostess for having a lovely time, etc., but it seems to work.

Make enough copies of legible handouts. There's nothing quite like coming up short with thirty-five strangers or having unfamiliar materials that no one can decipher.

It's better for the sub to take roll orally. For some reason students seem (really) to be put off by having their names mispronounced, but it's easy not to. Some names are not Mary and Jane but Geraldo (Hair-all-dough) and Nguyen = Win. It would be really helpful if phonetic or other symbols were used to explain pronunciations. Some Jeffrey's are now Jeff; Milton is nicknamed "Red" and he wants to be known as that. Jesus (hay-soos or Hey, Seuss) is now Chuy (Chewy to you).

Some last names are even more challenging. Try these names on for size: Cherniachowski (Chair-knee-uh-hof-shh-ski), Urtusuastegui (Err, like the Standard of Ur, 2 as in two, swaw-sta-gee, ghee or clarified butter), Brenot (long O, silent T), Inouye (Eeen-no-way with an emphasis on way), Jerkunica (Jerk-you-nick-a? NO!) (Yair-coo-neat-sa), Ciftcikara (Chift-chee-car-ah), and finally Branczeisz (Bran-size). "It's been shortened three times since we came from Hungary; no one could pronounce it before." (a student) Please tell us on your roll sheets and we can do it better.

Point out troublemakers with a symbol. A dot in front of a few names won't spoil the sheet. You're not pre-programming bad behavior; he's the same kid it took you, the regular teacher with power, more time and muscle to control and be with you; we'll find out who he is shortly anyway, but forewarned is better. Another option would be for you to put a 3 or a U, if those are the symbols you use for low citizenship grades, beside the names of students who deserve them.

I had a geography teacher tell me that he was going to give me "an easy day" (with my back turned to his class?). I was going to copy four columns of cities, rivers, and countries on the blackboard ("and leave it up for the next class-hour"). The students were going to free-hand copy the outlines of North America, then fill in all of this other information. (A real throwaway lesson.) I could "ask a student to do the copying on the board" if I wanted. We had two different atlases to work from and the information in one of them was not complete. Was that going to be an easy day?

The kids complained that they would like to have outline maps like all the other teachers gave their students. Those kids were feeling deprived by a neglectful parent. There were no seating charts; and the class environment degenerated until I said by chance, I think, to the girl who was my most obvious detractor, "I'm a guest in your school, and I don't think you're treating me very nicely!" I had dropped a bomb and I didn't know what had happened. That class clammed up; the mood changed perceptibly, and then I began to put together the idea of the classroom as family.

From the very beginning of your teaching career you have been trained to see everything that's going on in your classroom. Your power of observation has been honed on all kinds of body language that is often quite primary and you're aware of all sorts of nuances. You see the pimple on the girl's forehead, know it's that time of the month, and you don't pressure her for the new few days; keep it all low key and everyone feels better. When the stud and the blond chicky exchange knowing looks as the film describes the reproduction of the hibiscus, do you confront them with what you've seen; call their mothers? The old admonition against "telling tales out of school" is as valid today as it was in years gone by, apparently.

Your public emotions run somewhere between an "A" to perhaps an "E" (if you're a real "bitch" or "bastard"). You have to raise your voice only if the class situation is desperate. The rest of the time you're usually this really reasonable, sympathetic, subjective grade giver, who's nice to be with, is teaching things that are worth knowing about most of the time. You're always put together so that you don't look like that gross father with the stubble and bad breath that your students see first thing in the morning.

Can you imagine what sorts of things sometimes do happen in your students' happy homes? Read the police blotter section of the local paper and plug into the range of what's really happening out there in the face of unemployment, drunkenness, insecurity and resentment. Notice that some of the last names of those involved in public distress are those of current and ex-students and their families.

If something has gone wrong and when they come to apologize to you for transgressing some standard of acceptable behavior, you are an understanding and forgiving parent who never holds grudges. Perhaps something really horrendous happened at their house last night; they were not quite themselves. And it's a comfortable, warm relationship that includes all of these classmates. You're the kindly, rational parent. You have to be judgmental and totally objective, liberal and conservative, feeling and heartless, taking in and giving out but it's done quietly and just part of the way life is. It's a tough job. And remember you have a public and private character. Members of a family don't talk outside about one another, unless something that's really an outrage has happened, and the transgressor has to be publicly humiliated to stop that behavior. How many times has a teacher been reported at home for having said an accidental "damn" or "hell" in class? Nothing is to be said other than generalized topics.

Members of the family try to forgive the one who needs some more time to grow up, and our pressures on one another are usually gentle ones. I think that this is what is happening in most classrooms if the mix is right.

At one school, just before Christmas vacation, a girl's wallet was relieved of $60-$80, a lot of money to have been stolen, and perhaps her gift-giving fund. There had been few transients in the class that hour (an activity one). The students seemed stunned and unable to deal with the notion that one among them had been willing to steal from another. It was suggested that the money may have been taken for someone's survival, but that didn't seem to help.

In another school, after the lockers had been vandalized, one girl announced that she knew who had done it. When classmates insisted she tell the VP, she said, "I'm not a narc." But when she was asked, "Where are your loyalties to your fellow students?" she willingly went to the office.

The class wasn't quite like the normal stay-in-your-seats-during-the-classhour type. It was very free-flow and undemanding. It was part of a program to keep fringe dropouts to stay on and get as much knowledge and socialization for as long as possible. They have a separate facility across campus. I've subbed about five times with them; and they've just grown up faster than the norm of their age range; and they can't tolerate the childish games of the regular school. Emotionally they're quite immature.

Michelle was beautiful but bitchy; she was a model and physically an incredible specimen. To destroy totally that nice thought was her monstrous personality. She pouted, she crossed her arms over her chest frequently, she would stand and start swaying so that her hair could float back and forth (like a shampoo ad) to continuously draw attention to herself. She made some really nasty and caustic remarks to her female classmates like calling one girl "blubberbutt", another was questioned about why she "Always wore the same things every day?", another about why didn't she "take better care of your hair; it looks like a dishrag." One girl, talking about her, said, "It was rumored that the casting couch had nothing to do with her frequent modeling assignments."

During a film after the fifth or sixth, "This is boring"; a deep sigh, the humming of the first few bars of a song, the tapping of her feet, etc. — I had finally had enough. Without really thinking about my surrogate teacher status, I said rather loudly as I recall, "Dammit, Michelle, shut the Hell up!" It was a genuine teacher voice. Her body convulsed, and then she froze. She was out on a limb. I had cut her out of the herd.

She got up and flounced to the teacher's desk at the opposite corner and sat in the chair. After the film there was a discernible movement towards me. I gave the kids a ten minute rap on the topic presented in the film; the class listened respectfully and without moving. (Ordinarily, within fifteen seconds some girl would have asked her friend in an ordinary speaking voice to borrow her mascara, and they would have carried on a lively and continuing conversation on the wonders of lavender eye shadow.) A break was called. All the students left the classroom and not one went to console Michelle. She was all alone.

She was also a survivor. She met me halfway actually; and we chatted amiably and we smiled at one another. I think she'll lay off her classmates from now on, too. (Remember my admonition on don't ever say, "Shut up!" Usually, I don't.)

A teacher, who used the VP's name (the one in charge of discipline) in one example of the lesson, was startled when several students expressed concern that the teacher would "get into trouble" for having used the name. Correct the prepositional phrase for clarity: "Mr. Beech climbed the ladder with the broken arm." The VP, Mr. Beech, is not a member of the family.

And now, the sub enters that scene. How does he take

these orphans, whose parent has abandoned them today, and make them happy to be with him instead? Not with some of those killer lessons. Nobody's perfect, but some of those lessons have been murder, you guys.

Now, those kids are abandoned and they get a lesson that anyone would recognize for not only being totally out of sequence, that lesson obviously has no merit either, nothing is to be learned really; it's not going to get done, and the sub is going to spend his time as either a referee or ringmaster. Your lesson has guaranteed that.

Brenot's Iron Law of Probability: In each teaching career there has been at least one classroom without enough corners. To put that another way:

$$Given: the classroom$$
$$1x + (35y) = -z$$
$$teacher = x; students = y; corners = z$$

Please don't ask us to be experts: Discuss Chapter 7; discuss the Romantic Movement in literature; introduce fractions; show how $P40 - QR^2 = \frac{X}{VT} \neq 9$; lecture on how Dante and Machiavelli, Schumann and Strauss are not only interrelated but actually have synergistic relationships historically. Give the Dictee (use a Provencal accent, please) from l'Etranger, before you translate the passage from Verlaine (and please be especially sensitive to the nuances involved). How would you like to have been the substitute for Plato, Aristotle, Socrates, Buddha, Jesus, Moses, Mohammed, Mozart, Linus Pauling? We know you don't qualify, but it's better if you keep substitute lessons simple enough that someone who took the course twenty to forty years ago can muddle through it with even limited knowledge.

The teacher must be an expert in his subject area. He must really know what he's talking about, be interested in peripheral and related aspects of his subject, be aware of new technology, research, and directions; he must have a level of expertise that I didn't realize was necessary to conduct a high school class. Successful classes can't be bluffed; ask the

32

students about that.

Try to schedule as many field trips as possible. Allow some space in the budget for them. Students really enjoy a more relaxed and different kind of contact with the teacher away from the same old setting. Besides you would only take them to a place you know about and have enjoyed, otherwise you wouldn't have chosen that particular spot. Then you're really an expert in that topic and the student understands that classroom instruction is the same. You really know what you're talking about and can function whether it's basic instruction in school or in community and out in the real world. It's an important contact.

For standard academic classes sub lessons seem to need the following ingredients:

1. They must keep each student occupied and on his own. A sheet of paper must be given to each on which he puts his name.

2. They must have a time limitation for completion, at the latest the end of the hour.

3. They must be collected by the end of the hour.

4. They must be graded and that grade recorded. This may be only a ✓ +, ✓ , ✓ - or point credit assigned on a scale of one to ten, but it's vital that the lesson "count".

5. They must not be new material to the class, like introduce fractions, but a recapping, a co-alescing, a reinforcing of an already known subject area, perhaps with a new twist recombined to show new directions or ways of looking at the topic, or so self-contained that they teach themselves.

6. They must not be a continued lesson from yesterday. Too often the more disciplined or bored student will complete the lesson at home and be empty-handed that following day.

7. They must be structured so that someone who remembers only vaguely the topic from his own high school experience can supervise it. He may never have had an additional course in this area since then. You don't want your students to get misinformation. When misinformation is given in class, it's later correction is about as effective as a newspaper retraction on page 64, three weeks later. Even in your own field, the five minutes before class begins is not enough time to get a focus on the topic. You don't know what the teacher has emphasized already, where the information is supposed to go, what the objectives of that lesson are. Try it yourself sometime without notes and see how well you fare. Subs are babysitters, not teachers. Remember also that the sub has very limited use of the chalkboard. He can't turn his back on your students without the missiles lifting off instantly.

Please spare the sub those "discuss chapter 14" lesson plans. It's not reasonable. After getting out of the habit of repeating the same stuff for three hours running, there's nothing quite like it. For your students to have a stranger droning on and on for fifty minutes, no matter how lurid the examples used, it's not a very interesting class hour. I had to catch myself from saying at the end of the third session, "God, this is boring stuff!" It's just as well I didn't; for one range of student something like that said by any adult takes on the force of the gospel and as they are pretty unselective, often that negativism extends to other aspects as well. I could have done a great deal of damage inadvertently.

8. They must be slightly too long to finish ideally. The sub then can make a deal with your students at the end of the hour. He will ask you in a note to allow your students some little time to complete the lesson tomorrow. He will have collected it, but you will return it then. Have you ever heard of a teacher who would refuse to let his

little students complete a lesson? Besides, he's just returned to school and has a whole bunch of undone obligations to take care of. He's delighted to have some extra time. Too often the sub is asked, "May we go early? This is boring." I've never been in a classroom yet where everyone was vitally busy, when that question was asked.

Please teach me. Punch the Pronoun, Snap the Syntax, Grab the Godzilla, and Meditation Memories may be all right in their place, but I don't know where that is. I don't even know what you're talking about. I'm the person who's supposed to be in charge of your class today and I'm the only person in your classroom who doesn't know what those terms mean, what we're supposed to play. Please tell us in plain English. Translate the slang. It's not generally accepted English, you know, and effective communication was the standard you required on the papers you read and graded last night.

Please don't set the sub up for instant failure and your students for a terrible day. Your ego doesn't need it that badly. There are no easy days in the substitute racket. There have been some excellent and rewarding days, but they have never been easy. They have been the product of a lot of observation, trial and error (and a lot of that), and the application of the basic principles laid out here. Please consider seriously the hierarchy of lesson formats. The low numbers are the best.

The Hierarchy of Lessons:
1) Fill-in blank dittos. A self-contained packet with all instructions included. Example: conjugate to be, present tense, negative, interrogative, answer a series of questions using this information. The lesson was perfect. The teacher had done all of the work for me and all I had to do was be helpful to students while I circulated.

2) Read chapter 2 and answer questions 1-10. Curiously, this oldest of trite lessons is among the most effective.

35

3) To the library. Hazards — distance from the classroom to the library, the sub doesn't know your students so must take a second roll at the end of the hour, may be unfamiliar with the library himself and, therefore, not very helpful with your students. Usually, these are longer-term assignments that lack an immediate time commitment. If there is a paper due at the end of the class hour based on what was done, this is a good format.

4) Films or videos, but only if they are relevant and good ones. With a NOVA, I'm interested in science myself. There should be some written statement or series of questions to accompany it. Have a backup just in case of power failure.

5) A writing assignment. This is effective only if the group is college prep and highly motivated. Even then the hazard here is time.

6) Lecture — In general, avoid it; but it should not extend beyond a very few minutes at the most.

7) Student oral reports, projects, demonstrations, geomety proofs. The problem here is grading. There is so much subjective criteria included, and we don't know your students, what it will take to keep them encouraged and productive. We just think that the presentation is superficial, emotional, not learned, hasty, not very informative. That's only one side of this kid's effort, but that's all we see.
For a geometry proof lesson the teacher had the students put their work on the board; I had the key and made corrections when a step had been omitted. That worked out really well. But I still didn't know how to mark the grade proportionally to the number of omissions.

8) Oral questions and answers. Without very detailed instructions, unless this is the sub's field of expertise, this may be a bomb. Someone who knows little about the topic chews through a lot of information and data, too much usually for students to absorb.

9) Group work. If there is a time deadline and

students can see the purpose of their working together rather than separately, this can work pretty well. Generally, there's a lot of goofing off, irrelevant (to the topic) conversation about almost anything else, and little accomplished. The most dedicated students usually do the assignment for the others and she's usually female.

10) Read chapter 2. That's it. Why embellish a good thing? If it works, don't fix it; but it doesn't.

11) Have students do a review for the test tomorrow, or read their novels.

12) Let the students browse through the magazines and find an interesting article to read . . .

For activity classes the problems are different. In general the closest that this day resembles one while the regular teacher is there, the better. That's okay for drama, cooking and sewing, dance, art; ceramics is riskier; but welding and woodshop, chem. lab impossible. (I've not tried performing or vocal music classes.) Often this is the reward at the end of the day class for low-enders and they're not too pleased that the sub doesn't know enough about the topic to allow them to do the very activity that they enjoy the best, has made school tolerable at all, and that they've looked forward to all day. Almost inevitably the welding and woodshop instructors have sent an assignment which requires reading from a textbook or manual with some writing or fill-in work to be completed. Goodie! Their favorite lesson style. The sub can let this work for him by being "helpful." For low-enders reading is often difficult, writing more so, and if the sub helps them with those difficult tasks, they appreciate that and that partially counteracts the negative factor of his not knowing how to weld.

To the Substitute:

Keep your explanations simple and concise; be calm and brief. They appreciate your aid. Don't do it all; they're often good con artists, too. Keep them away from all of that expensive and dangerous machinery. Some of those kids can move pretty fast. Be prepared for the worst at all times when you're with these kids.

If there is a movie or filmstrip following a written lesson, that's even better. It must be instructive, not frivolous. You've got to strike for love here, not fear of your non-authority. I had an irate father glaring at me for the whole classhour. He was required by the school to attend all classes one day with his son who had unilaterally declared a series of school holidays. The father's response was a law and order approach to his problem (even though that hadn't worked out too well so far, obviously). I'm sure he didn't realize what I was experimenting with and trying to do.

For a low-end activity class the last ten minutes is their usual clean up time. If you have been sent some sort of bookwork assignment to do, put in a ten minute filler or rap with them. Otherwise they'll get out of their seats and increase the probability that some sort of damage might be done; or a few may escape your clutches. You'll avoid that by shifting gears.

Even though the first time I had become Susie Homemaker, the happy cooker, everything had gone so well it took a second type of assignment to make me aware of another needed lesson. Rather than the cooking groups in the class each preparing "the recipe of the day" that had worked out so well before, I or some students were to do a demonstration lesson instead. I had already learned that a sub especially should never become a dancing seal or preoccupied with doing something himself; but rather must be free to circulate and make contact with strangers and calm down any hot spots with his presence.

The girls who had been chosen to do the demonstration, not at all trained to do presentations, mumbled to themselves and generally lost their audience early in the game. I tried to fill in the holes but it wasn't working. Baking time was twenty-five minutes and resting time an additional ten (out of a fifty minute classhour). There was too much dead time for a sub to sustain without some alternative or supplementary activity to fill the void. The last straw for that class was the discoery that the oven hadn't been turned on. No sample of this dish at the end of the hour. There was

38

a general bolt for the exit; I was lucky to lose only four, three of whom came back later. Of course, I assigned detention.

For activity classes the best lesson seems to be the one which occupies each student directly, keeps his hands busy ("idle hands are the devil's work"), and attention focused on a specific task which has some completion. Sewing classes later that day took care of themselves and were very pleasant. When I explained that I didn't know how to sew with a machine (I learned to darn socks and sew on buttons in the Army, I explained), students would say nice things like, "That's too bad; they're offered at the community college, you know. It's fun to do."

If there is to be a demonstration, cooking or baking time ought to be quite short, or enough supplementary activities introduced to fill any void. One home economics teacher uses dead time for introducing tomorrow's lesson, has a short vegetable chopping session for tomorrow's preparation, gives students information on nutrition, teaches them how to set a formal dinner table. Dead time activities might include a section on decorating cakes or a whole house, care of indoor plants, the value of a marketing list, menu plan for leftovers, how to use tiny amounts of meat to stretch carbohydrates almost forever, and casserole cookery or how to stretch it even farther with a sauce. The possibilities are endless.

It was interesting having two hours of co-ed P.E. During one classhour, when touch football teams were totally integrated, everything went beautifully. Each gender seemed to automatically respect the others' strengths and limitations. They were really having a good time together and it felt right. It was like a Sunday game at a park or the beach. The next classhour I was cautioned that the boys were too rough and the teams were to be separated. The boys divided into 4 teams and got at it almost instantly. The girls had 2 enormous teams, dawdled, argued, got angry, frustrated, and I had to referee an absolute charade of an exercise session to get it moving at all. The natural athletes took the game over and the more retiring ones tuned out and barely went through the motions.

Later their instructor told me that he too spent every

day with the girls' teams, supervising and refereeing differences. I wondered if he had ever considered letting a co-ed team form voluntarily for those who would prefer it, and maintain separated ones for the others. The classes were large enough to make that possible.

A problem group for the sub in almost every P.E. class is the non-athletic type who would do anything to get away from all of that sweaty activity. "Be sure not to sweat too much" was the way one boy put it. They're rarely dressed; they forgot their gym clothes; their lawyer fathers can't afford them right now; they have been menstruating continuously for the past thirty-six months. The excuses take all forms for P.E. Really all the sub can do is report the student to the teacher on the capsule of the day sheet unless there is a point system being used. Then the sub can assign either zero or negative points.

Skip-outs are another primary problem so it's wise to announce at the very beginning of the classhour that another roll will be called at the end of the hour. You'll need about five minutes for this so stop the play early and they'll not miss shower time.

Shower time is a love-hate relationship. A lot of them don't like to expose their bodies to one another completely; on the other hand they don't like to feel sweaty and hot either. The school district could put in some baffles but no school I've ever been to has thought of that apparently. (Incidentally, unless there's some supervision reason, as a sub stay out of the locker room. You're not a member of the family and you ought not be there.)

When the three boys vaporized from the P.E. class and sneaked into the pool area next door, did they paddle quietly so they wouldn't be noticed? Not with a sub there they didn't; they were jumping off the high diving board and yelling, "Geronimo" so that no one could miss it. They were counting on anonymity and the loyalty of their classmates not to divulge their names and no one did. I nabbed them with a second roll but to avoid the problem of not easily knowing names of students in gym classes, students might be required to have their last names printed in block letters on the rear of their gym shorts. Even if they're running away, you get a second chance; and few kids will want to take off their shorts to avoid detection. (Incidentally, don't laugh

40

when kids do things you think personally are hilarious; they're not aware of legal liabilities and classroom control problems; even though you know they're just having some fun at your expense, don't laugh. It encourages that kind of behavior if you do).

Incidentally, keep your hands off students, too. A handshake is one thing, but almost any body contact other than that carries its own risk. Don't do it. Punishing physically is, of course, illegal (in California at least and should be nationwide); but other forms of contact can be easily misunderstood.

As a rule of thumb don't be in a classroom with a lone single student of the opposite sex for a protracted time. It sometimes happens as a result of field trips and activity periods. Make some excuse like, "I've got to talk to the librarian," and go there. The student will probably be less bored in the library than anywhere else that's neutral. At least you haven't foisted him off on the ceramics teacher or another catch-all activity classroom.

Subbing is incredibly manipulative, Pavlovian — Machiavellian. It's babysitting with a twist. They're not babies anymore. Teaching is much more subtle and really an art. One of your primary jobs is to counteract all of the negative associations with a sub day and continue, much as usual, the warm and comfortable family atmosphere already created by the teacher, (or in some cases counteract as well as you can the bad atmosphere already created). That's more difficult and takes longer, several days. You're stuck as ringmaster for a single day.

These seem to be the major concerns that students have on sub days:
a)   They're afraid that something they do may not be graded; if it doesn't count, why do it? And if the sub has the ability to determine that grade, he has even more power.
b)   They're afraid of "trouble", punishment, being kicked out of class, assigned detentions, sub *power*.
c)   They're afraid that the sub can't keep the class under control; they will have a day with a lot of emotional chaos and miss the nice contacts in the class that day.

41

d)   They're afraid that their time may be wasted and the lesson not continued with a sub there.

Some have said that they like to have a *new face* now and then and a potential *new approach* in class. They would like to have a kindly aunt or uncle type be with them for a day or so.

When the boy said in response to my "How do you feel when you see a sub?" question, "Now we have to break someone else in." I had heard that as break down, I guess, as I thought it was a threat to me. At that time it never occurred that the reverse was what he may have meant and that he had felt threatened as a student.

Collette Cunningham had been absent for three days and she paled when there was an unfamiliar face on her return to school. It took her exactly three sentences to tell me that despite a) her appearance which said otherwise (she was into her modified rock-a-billy phase), she lived in one of the more exclusive gated areas of town; b) her father was "in medicine"; and c) she considered herself a serious student. Self-image, self-importance, ego, security, the whole lot may be seriously imperiled with a sub.

An aspect of substitute control will be to respect that and reassure students. The teacher does or should do that every day and the sub must try to sustain the continuity of the good, the ideal teacher but must counteract or compensate for the flawed, less than ideal teacher. And many teachers are flawed, but no profile of what teacher type he is subbing for is given to the sub along with the keys and the day's assignment. It is up to a substitute's quick perception to judge the atmosphere and student attitude and to be able to compliment or countervail the pre-established atmosphere if the day is to go smoothly and productively.

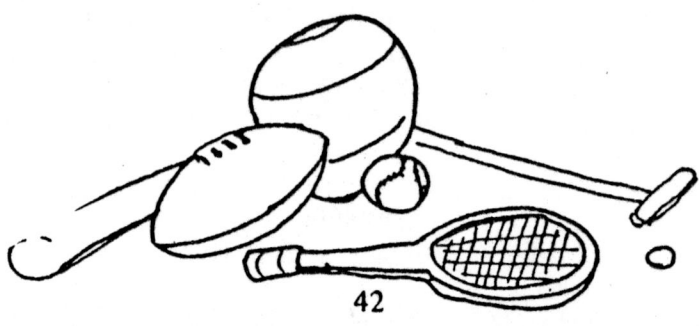

Up until now we've been talking almost exclusively about pigeons and monkeys, about them and students and that was more comfortable. This section deals with people called us and ours and their differences, some of their characteristics. That may tend to make us more defensive and uncomfortable in facing some of the harsh realities of schools and public education. These are trickier shoals.

Some Teacher Profiles: Who are some of these people who are teaching our children?

So many of her reactions seemed unusual. At a faculty meeting when teachers were battling over a philosophical issue, she said, "Here we sit like so much unthinking popcorn" She said that at home her neighbors were tunneling under her patio; she said that Myrna Loy (an actress from the original "Thin Man" series of the late 30's) had come to her house to borrow some long dresses for a party; she said that at school carrot and celery sticks were being stolen out of a locked refrigerator by the janitors every night (some wag estimated that they must be the healthiest custodians in town with that diet). She brought the biology teacher a very live and coiled rattler. She had stunned it earlier in her driveway by hitting it with a frying pan; had dumped it in the trunk of her car, and had brought it as a special surprise. She said that she had been married once at the Little Church Around the Corner (bend or over the hill) in New York off 5th Avenue. He had left her at the altar after the ceremony was over and she had never seen him again. She was always headed up the off ramp and coming out of the entrance; up the down staircase and in the exit. She always seemed to be out there looking in at the others doing their strange things. Every time the cookies burned it was the first time ever. She had a terrible driving record. Her approaches were just not the usual, standard ways of looking at the world. She taught for more than thirty years.

However, her sage advice at her retirement party was, "If you do it wrong once or twice at the beginning, they won't ask you to do it any more; and you get out of a lot of work that way." That was certainly appropriate.

He had a reputation for never smiling; kids called him Happy Harry; his moral code was rigid and inflexible; he "was boring"; students hated him and dreaded his classes. "I don't make the rules; I just enforce them" seemed to be his favorite expression despite the lessons of the Nuremberg Trial. As he got older he mellowed out considerably. He began to smile; and miraculously, his students began to like him better and fewer of them described his classes as boring.

He was pretty erratic but a nice man himself, but "he just let students run all over him"; students complained that "they didn't learn anything in his classes". They wished he would "tighten up". Some even opted to take "the demanding, petty, and unfair" alternative teacher instead.

The teacher's husband is an efficiency expert for an electronics firm. He has established a reputation for being very good in his field. He determined that since electronic parts didn't need to be kept warm in the warehouse, it would cut expenses considerably if the heat were turned off there. The warehousemen worked faster because it was so cold and uncomfortable, and he could eliminate a few of them because of this increased efficiency.

He kept a locked gas cap on his daughter's car and that would discourage any excessive driving as she would be constantly aware of her mileage.

Every time the husband cut back on something else at home, his wife went out to buy a lot of new clothing for herself; every time he left town on a business trip, she bought herself champagne, filet mignons, lobster and scallops. They had macaroni and cheese and meatloaf meals when he was at home. One day she was absent from school. Some students mixed all of the photographic developing chemicals together and ruined tham all. Who did that? The students closest to the teacher, her confidants, of course.

After hearing about this little warehouse manipulation, I wonder about some of those slimy liquid hand soaps with hand lotion included that take a lot more water and many more towels to get your hands to feel clean or dried off. I wonder who worked that one out for his fun and profit? I have reconsidered the advice to the thrifty housewife who is told to use cold water when running the garbage disposal also. If enough grease gets coagulated and stuck in the mechanism, then how much faster does the disposal burn out, and how much more profit do the manufacturers of disposals make?

When the teacher said that his private self was a totally different package from his public one, I really didn't think much about that at the time. But how can that be? Aren't we schizophrenic if we have two distinct ways of looking at ourselves and our surroundings? That couldn't be possible among normal, everyday teachers of the youth of our country, now could it?

The teacher's wife is old enough to be his mother. She owns some apartments. He keeps porno magazines under their bed. They have no children. His teaching role model had been a very pretentious and pseudo-learned middle-aged man who married one of his 18 year old students.

At a parent conference after the father had gotten tearful about his only son who wanted to be a marine mechanic (the father had just gotten custody of the boy after a 7 year court struggle), the teacher sat back with steepled fingers and related the time on January 7th when the boy had failed to turn in his homework assignment and other major crimes.

This older mate/wife, pot smoker, outwardly free-liver changed the color of her eye shadow after reading a narcisistic book about color compatibility based on skin tone. They seem so inconsistent.

Her body seems to be in perfect proportion despite all of the padding. She's summer; he's a winter. They are compatible and physical. She runs and works out daily. He is studly. They're young, vibrant, handsome, boring, unattractive and scary. They're from Detroit. She's been cold ever since they arrived in California so she wears long johns, two pairs of heavy socks under denim pants, two chemises under a pink silk blouse, some gold chains to keep her chest warm. They're both diamonds in the rough actually and a little insecure. He smiles a lot; she nibbles on a carrot stick, a celery stick and then has two almonds. They don't eat dinner. They seem consumed with appearances. He has announced a series of skiing weekends. She's not expected to go because of the cold.

She's in her mid-forties, has never been married, lives with her mother in a comfortable middle-range housing development. Her mother takes care of the house, the cooking, their clothing. The daughter can't "cook her way out of a paper bag", but does the small amount of gardening necessary as a recreation.

The teacher loves cats. Her classroom is literally coated with pictures of cute little baby animals, cute little human babies with cute little sayings attached to each one. There are stalactites of a dozen or so mobiles hanging from the ceiling. Assignments are written out on a corner of the blackboard and they give details like, "Review the language assignment the last five minutes of class." The teacher's desk has been placed strategically behind her students, and she spends most of the classhour there. She assigns detention for the most minor student misbehavior and is considered a model teacher by the administration, because, as one fellow teacher noted, "The only sound you ever hear from her classroom is the scratching of chalk on her blackboard."

She has lunch alone, except for days when there are departmental meetings. She always flees from those early.

A third year teacher who had devised a very complicated point system for determining grades, suddenly announced one day to her classes that she had cancelled out on that structure (effective several weeks before) and was replacing it with a simpler method. When asked why by her students, she answered, "When you get as old as I (25), you're entitled to change your mind." Her classes have been bedlam ever since; can you imagine that?

Her classroom is a scattered jumble of animal posters, a few cartoons, books covered with cloths for some reason, a lot of little stuff all over the place.

She has constructed an effective barricade by putting her desk, which has a tall out-in box, a tall stationery organizer, an extra tall box of Kleenex, next to a lectern; then a long work table with a stool behind it. She has put pieces of tape on the floor so that student desks cannot creep forward toward her, and she maintains this buffer zone of guaranteed space dividing her from her students.

It's amazing how tolerant students are of their teachers.

Some Teacher Types

That old adage to the new teacher of don't smile before Thanksgiving or laugh before Christmas directly contradicts the reality of the classroom. You can catch more flies with honey than vinegar and many more students with love is a neglected topic of the school relationship. You can't scare a kid into learning anything (except fear, perhaps). You can and do manipulate him by a series of stratagems into leaving his house so that he will enter yours to learn.

The nice stable classroom where students are contented and serene, they know what to expect from their teacher; he's all together himself, not some Jekyll-Hyde type, is the easy one for the sub to manage and feel confident in.

On the heels of the faulty lesson these are the really hard acts for the sub to follow. They complicate our lives quite a bit.

"The atmosphere is like a roller coaster. We get used to having quiet times but then everything breaks out in a violent discussion. We get used to those sharp changes." (a student) As a sub get used to the wild swings and ups and downs in this sort of classroom. Try to counteract them or divert student attention with your calmness.

"You're not going to be graded on how well you play, but on your effort. That's bullshit!" (a student commenting on the declared basis for grading in his P.E. class)

"We spent most of our time trying to avoid what he was making us do."

"I have a feeling of being in prison in this class."

"When we have a decent teacher, we don't know how to act."

The Authoritarian or Contentious Teacher:

When the shop teacher called out "Clean up", the kid just sat there and ignored him. The teacher walked over, grabbed the boy's shirt front, lifted him off his stool and said, "When I say clean up, I mean now." The kid hopped to.

When someone in the class was unruly, a standing choice was given for punishment. Either the illegal paddle was administered (a wide one like those the teacher had used years before in Ohio schools, not narrow like a ruler which would leave a tell-tale welt; the teacher wood-burned the names of the kids into the paddle, like so many notches in a gun). Or the kid could take his chances in the dreaded office. A referral there usually meant expulsion because of this teacher's reputation. And that meant trouble at home, too.

Question: What if you as a sub are not as physically imposing as this teacher? How do you think students will act that hour if someone with a different style is the sub? In either case you lose, sucker. That guy has preprogrammed disasterous days for a sub. Only the best structured lesson could save you from a terrible day; even then, have your whip ready because you're going to be using it. Only later, on subsequent visits, can you ever add gentleness and helpfulness. That's after students begin to know and trust you as someone who's different.

Often the contentious teacher has a sizeable proportion of every class made up of assertive-aggressive types who seem to demand control from him. He obliges them with a strong arm; he tends to be rigid and rule-imposing, demanding, fear inducing; he has developed a strident manner;

there seems to be constant struggle, underground warfare, and agitation in class.

Students also complain that this type is patronizing and constantly talks down to them. They see him as a delayed adolescent himself who needs a lot of attention. His ego needs constant stroking. Student opinions and discussion are held in low regard as this teacher tells them what to think from his fountain of all-knowing correct information. Students have said that they feel that he looks on them as unimportant, young and inexperienced and, therefore, having little or no validity. Students would like a reciprocal interchange and some warmth from this type. Teaching is also the art of listening.

It has typically taken the teacher some time to settle these groups down and he feels that he can't "let up". He can and should. He needs to turn the atmosphere of that group (ever so gradually) into one of love and a family, and *force* those kids to be glad to be there with him. Students usually "don't like him, particularly" up to absolute hate because he's "sort of erratic" and "he can't be counted on."

When the contentious teacher is away, some of his lower-end students especially (who misconstrue the non-contentious manner of a sub) will misbehave. They will be less likely to misbehave for a contentious sub. The next obvious step to solve that little dilemma is to match the contentious teacher with an appropriate sub to match his style. It would be less shock and adjustment for those classes. The risk here is a mis-match. Imagine the atmosphere of a class with a contentious sub and a reasaonable bunch of students! They'll complain vehemently that the sub was a bitch/bastard. Firm discipline is not contentiousness. Contentiousness is childish hostility. self-indulgence, ego gratification, and a fear of not being in control.

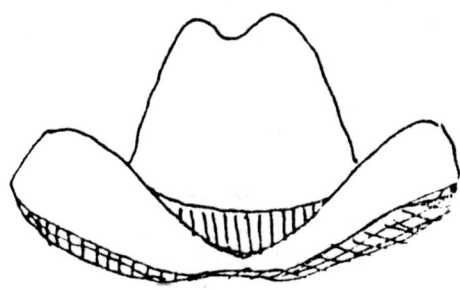

49

The First Year Teacher:

He may not be actually but may as well be. He hasn't learned the most basic lesson about teaching kids and that is that you can't be selfish and deny your students your affection and regard, concern, interest, respect, and warmth.

He may still feel that moment of panic, when after the contract signing and the initial elation, he realized that he had just committed himself to facing classrooms of younger strangers so many hours per day, five days a week.

How many new teachers may have said to themselves some variation on this theme? I hate teenagers; but I've invested time, a lot of effort, and quite a bit of daddy's hard-earned money on this venture. It's a mistake, but I can't back out now. I'm stuck with it, at least for the time being.

He is still vaguely afraid of his students, the administration, his supervising teacher, the department chairman, the parents, even the custodian who may report to the VP in charge of whatever that he consistently has a lot of paper and mess in his classroom and is, therefore, incompetent. He is one to five days ahead of his students in the text and worries that someone may ask a question that he can't answer. He is afraid that someone is going to find out that he is a fraud; not a teacher at all, just a lonely and scared person trying to make his daily living by misrepresenting his capacity to teach anything to anyone, ever.

Sometimes he does an erratic Red Queen routine, and it's off with their heads; otherwise, he usually puts up with too much student misbehavior because he really doesn't want to call attention to himself in the office by too frequent referrals. And so his classes fall apart.

He feels inferior and is. His students see him as weak and flawed and treat him with contempt and derision. They sense that he's not even in control of himself. They really dislike him. He has terrible control. These people need to learn how to relax, take themselves less seriously, and gain a much needed regard for their students.

He's often a cold fish. He's "boring". He lectures for the whole classhour; he puts the assignments on the board or on a ditto and retires behind his desk to grade papers. Students don't like his classes. He builds his barriers against them quite effectively. He must also learn to vary the diet of presentation.

He also doesn't need to hate or fear teenagers. They can't help it if they aren't adults yet; give them another four years. New teachers just have to adjust to where their students are, not join them, but be aware of where they're coming from.

Now unfortunately, this is the very perception that a lot of students have for substitutes also. You must counteract that through body language and a gentle smile from the very beginning. You will have to sit down hard (use a two-by-four if necessary) at the very beginning to catch their attention; then gentle the atmosphere down but do that as rapidly as possible as students seem to feel comfortable with that layer of change. It may take a second or third visit before you can do the gentling; but when it happens, you'll *feel* the relaxation in this classroom.

The Educational Amoeba:

These are the guys who make your jellyfish look like King Kong in heavy action. They're educational magpie/ amoebas; they're most likely fascinated by the potentialities of the left-right brain analysis of learning style currently; they flow with the tide, and are often soon aboard the next bandwagon.

They tend not to want to hassle their students with a lot of unnecessary demands and structure. Learning is the key and that is done most effectively through self-motivation and encouragement. They try to be non-judgmental but are forced by the realities of the system to go along with things as they are. They would prefer learning environments rather than a standard classroom. They expect their students to pursue individual or group contractual independent inter-reactional programmed library and research oriented projects which often isolate the student from the teacher and from the total dependence on the teacher that most students have in the average classroom. He prefers keeping his classroom presentations short and infrequent, and the sub is an obvious interloper. Kids misbehave for different reasons.

In other words, all hard acts to follow seem to be people who tend to be either somewhat cold personally and/ or somewhat isolated from their students.

51

The amoeba will repeat Barry Goldwater's "right to fail" line. Don't expect to pass the course if you haven't done something that would make that appropriate. I can lead you to water but can't make you learn. I can lead you to knowledge, but can't make you think. I can try beating you to death, but you're going to learn only about fear and compulsion that way. What you learn is up to you. I'm here as another resource and guide. You come to me when you decide what you want to learn about and I'll help you.

Freshmen and underclassmen rebel and often cause real discipline problems for this emotionally detached teacher. They can't handle being either that starved for warmth or contact from a parental figure. Often students in this age group, individually and as a group, are contentious themselves (the control in junior high and so far in most other high school classes is based on not sparing the rod) that they don't know how to deal with a reasonable human being. They see the emotionally detached teacher as weak because he doesn't want to bother just doing discipline all day. He's got some other things on his mind.

Later on for upper classmen, many of these can relate to this approach really comfortably as they seek room for independent examination of their world. They're not as dependent any more on parental warmth as that is usually being supplemented with a first love.

The younger kids hate this teacher; the older and more mature ones usually adore him.

Be assertive to aggressive initially as necessary to catch their attention. Don't do an overkill, but be plenty firm. Then become gentler as you feel student acceptance. That first day may be tough, but the word spreads rapidly and you'll start getting some better relationships going a little later on.

Try always to be firm, and fair, and consistent.

Even though the educational amoeba is a hard act to follow for a sub, his teaching style is probably the very best for redirecting and reorienting student self-confidence. In the educational amoeba's class the student is able to pursue some individual project on his own and actually learn something in the process. The problem for the sub is that so much of the rest of the school is run on a contentious basis that the amoeba teacher is the odd-man-out, not the norm.

52

I asked students to list the contentious teachers in one school, and they ticked off at least 20 percent of the faculty members almost instantly and automatically.

The educational amoeba may be a magpie but at least he's willing to try something different that may work; that's better than sticking with systems that are known losers.

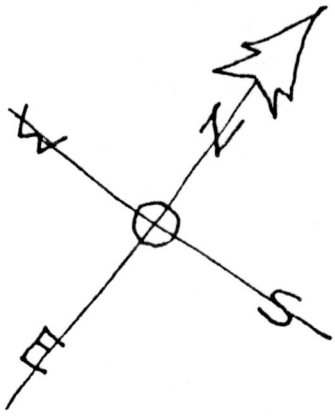

What Are Students Like?

Every teacher at some point in his career, not infrequently the first day, has had at least one student tell him, not openly (they aren't zero-basers; they're serious students) but by his general attitude and lack of effort and achievement (the student doesn't hold anything against the teacher personally either, mind you) that the kid simply *hates* the course; it's boring, dull and irrelevant. And maybe it is, to differing kinds of students.

Math-science students seem to like classes in which there is an orderly progression from point one through five. They don't seem to want a lot of flights of fancy, conjecture, what if's; they tend to want answers for things, not paradoxes. They like to categorize and theorize (not fantasize). They seem to get restless if the lesson, the general topic, the usual curriculum choice includes too much that is perceived as inexact, not defined, frivolous, and, therefore, irrelevant to know. They tend to like specifics and factual data (which they then like to contest). They feel comfortable being graded by the A–F (1–10) scales as a reasonable gauge of their achievement. They often see humanities types as a bit flaky and fuzzy-headed.

As an example only, they might like Home Economics classes better if the teacher would discuss the various chemical changes that take place when you add an egg now or later, separated, added intact or prebeaten, etc. They won't expect specific chemical formulas, just some reminders like, "There's nothing to cooking; it's just the science of putting things together and the chemical interaction of those ingredients."

Something is written, "with certain exceptions" for the math-science mind; but as, "there are other ways of looking at things" for a humanities orientation. If you need a student aide, choose a math-science type. They will get things organized, will grade simple assignments accurately, and be genuinely helpful. I plead the fifth on those others, but they can do inspired bulletin boards. Math-science people seem to want to list things and put them into straight lines; whereas, the humanities type often tends to have a circularity of thought pattern and action, too.

The humanities type, however, often hates math-science classes; usually, up to algebra and general science are okay, but after that it's too specific. There's nothing that then often seems to turn these kids off more than a year of geometry. They feel they don't need a whole year of logic; all the fine points of triangle ABD are so much ho-hum. Don't expect a humanities type to learn very much from a programmed text, or to buy a computer. They are more focused on historical antecedents, discovering relationships between one movement and another, discovering fully and refining their own libidos, as well; they don't want to be constantly concerned with the parts of things that make up something larger and orderly; they want to let their imaginations go and gain some interesting and, for them, new insights on what has made it all go or come together. They will predictably like language classes better if the teacher takes some time out from the drills, vocabulary, and exercise sessions and shows a few slides and talks about life in the old country and his personal experiences there. They often want to be graded on a pass-fail basis (✓+, ✓ , ✓-) as they feel that that is specific enough to gauge their effort. They often see math-science students as "very smart", but underneath feel that they're somehow dull and unimaginative. "Why does the clock always seem to stop in math class?" (a student)

The literary trinity of this, this, and that, a series of three, is usually treated as a sacred object by a humanities person. It seems necessary for the rhythmic patterning and cadence — the flow, but then that must be very irritating for the more linear approach of a math-science orientation. I've tried to break up that patterning here and there even though it has bothered me to do that.

"*The Star Wars* was all in the future". . ."Well, that's not really accurate; it's written in the past, but it's the past of the future, and that past is still in our future." One detractor said, "He's crazy; I don't understand what he says." Another detractor said, "I don't understand you." The boy who made the statement said, "Just forget it."

That's the test question to determine whether you've been paying attention to your lessons. Which type of student orientation probably would have made that statement?

During the course of a classhour, why not consider something for everybody. About twenty to thirty minutes into a class time, even though they've have a read and answer the questions lesson, even the best students are going to get restless. So join 'em and say, "Stop now, please; and let's review the points you might have listed to answer question one." Hopefully, most students will have completed that much anyway, so you're giving them nothing for free, actually. It will just seem that way to them. (Be sure to have read the questions to them at the first, so that they know more precisely what's being looked for.) Give them a listing one, two, three after you have done a quick skim yourself. They'll appreciate the "help" and you can then have them go on. Don't help them any more except one by one (and then only a little) as you circulate. Some kids may try to become dependents; don't let it happen.

Incidentally, the reason for the statistical sheet at the beginning of the handbook, printed out in two different styles, is that the first is a humanities style and the second is designed for a math-science orientation.

My mother-in-law said, "I don't like the statistical first page. It lacks perspective; put it into focus. It needs something." Why? Because she's a mean old woman who was trying to make me feel terrible; but despite that, because she is an almost pure math-science type and I, an almost pure humanities type. My wife who is some of both (a split personality) rewrote it for the handbook from a math-science approach. (She'd probably be a good doctor.) I just felt that the text needed a good or bad mother-in-law joke at this point; we get along really well; after twenty-two years she's learned to be forgiving.

Test yourself. Reread the statistical page and see which style gives you more information than the other. That would determine your basic learning orientation. The first is the humanities text approach and the second, a listing to satisfy the math-science need for concrete order.

Another way of looking at the high school experience is through the growth of an individual's maturity level. All of those incoming little individuals have come from the very contentious junior high school savage reservation we were warned about. The girls may have started puberty somewhere in the mid-eighth grade, but the typical incoming freshman boy is an obnoxious little brat. He's just one step away from having carried a favorite toy car to school to play with, and is loud, and jittery, and wildly erratic.

One of the constraints on this group is often a conspiracy of upper classmen who might dump one of these sub-species fully clothed into the pool, put him head first into a garbage can, pants him or perform some other deserved retribution for his being where he is in his maturation pro-cess. About the mid-point of his freshman year, something begins to happen; and by the end of his freshman year, he's a changed person and is becoming human despite himself. Usually then, by the beginning of the sophomore year, the bulk of that class is operating at a more adult level of be-havior.

Unfortunately, the constraint system of the school goes on with business-as-usual rather than adjusting to the new reality of the enormous strides that each student is going to make each year during his tenure in high school. It creates a continuation of the degenerating atmosphere for the stu-dent who is genuinely a young adult in age only. This large group perceives school constraints as being totally out of the realm of the real world. By the way, how many adults have to raise their hands to speak, or get permission to go to the bathroom? Many of them feel their time is being wasted with impractical baby-stuff and want to get on with the business of living their own lives, and developing their own skills in an atmosphere that reflects the practices of the real world. This process may explain, at least partially, the terribly high drop-out rate among high school students.

The order of the various segments is really irrelevant and that's why it's been so difficult to try to put the parts into a logical sequence. You must still read the total of the handbook to understand how to substitute, with whom, under what circumstances. Nevertheless, it's better if we now have a minor recess from how to do whatever and discuss a couple of institutions that are built right into the school environment.

To the Teacher:

You're really not going to want to hear this, much less think that it could be even possibly or partially true. It's hard to tell you after all of those years in which those students loved you for yourself alone, and certainly not for what you could do for them, that your estimations may have been a trifle off.

Times have changed! What used to be called sycophantism, elbow-shrining, apple-polishing, con-artistry, sucking-it-up, brown-nosing, ass-kissing, is now called star-fucking (*Mommie Dearest* by Christina Crawford defined this term.) And it's a real part of teaching. There are a lot of fragile egos out there that get soothed every day. But what is given is often taken away too by references to the size of your nose, the size of your salary in relation to his father's, the supermarket checker. There is none of this soothing for a sub first. But it doesn't take many visits to the same school to set the process in motion.

Consider this example from *Choices* by Thelma Altshuler, a compilation of interesting paradoxes including moral ones, page 132, number 3. "A teacher asks a student for a frank evaluation of a course he has taught for the first time. The person he asks has an average of B, on the borderline of being an A. Does the student mention what is wrong with the course content or the method of presentation?" Not one student I've queried has ever chosen to be honest and tell the teacher the truth.

An entry in a student's English journal: "P.E. is my favorite class because I love sports very, very much. English is probably my second favorite class because you're so nice and you make the work fun unlike other teachers who just lay the work out and don't care how long the work takes. Plus in English I like writing stories."

Now how many of you opt for considering this quotation as (a) a genuine expression of the student's fondness for this class or, (b) a blatant example of out-front star-fucking?

Remember that P. T. Barnum only said his rather famous sucker born every minute line after he, himself, had been bamboozled into walking miles to see the two-headed, talking dog; the one who answered his own questions.

Most students, however, are ardent star-fuckers; especially if they feel unsure of their own capabilities, or are heavily over-extended in time commitments and must make some shortcuts. Most are survivors; they won't close doors unnecessarily and tell you what they really think, because even years and years later, that may come back to haunt them; and they don't leave exposed flanks if they can help it. What they're doing is not always purposeful and calculated and not intended to cause any harm; they're simply pragmatists who are realistic in the way people operate; e.g., act more favorably toward, give allowances for, give the benefit of the doubt to those who flatter them. It's effective P.R.

My wife, the child of a teacher, was sent birthday, Christmas and Easter cards and lavished with all sorts of other little attentions for the entire four years that two students spent in the high school where her mother taught.

There are also star-fucking parents and power mad ones, too. There are even those who go so far as to "serve" on the Board of Education about the time their children are in school, but rapidly lose interest in the problems of public education almost immediately after their last child has graduated from high school.

It's difficult to be a surrogate parent all day to 150 or so children with whom you have varying degrees of rapport and empathy. Sometimes the best you can do is to barely tolerate, at other times you feel a genuine warmth for this child. Here's a pitfall. As a general rule despite everything, teachers, like actors, are notoriously poor judges of character. How do you recognize the little playactor who is laying on a lot of star-fuck? You don't if he's consistent enough. You are so vulnerable and gullible because you really do need to believe his siren. And some of these kids are star performers themselves..

The sub often sees these responsible, reliable, class teacher's-pets in a wholly different light, especially if the student doesn't feel that it's necessary to maintain the charade with the teacher gone. It can be a very difficult situation for the sub to have to punish (the demonstrator, class leader, editor, etc.) with detention after he essentially has led the class, no matter how badly and destructively, I need to add. Sometimes this student is *the* instrument for a class going badly. I can't think of a way to make classroom teachers more selective and evaluate these types more accurately.

Students are survivors; the brighter ones don't want to close any doors. Actually this little reality can work for the sub in the nicest ways if you take the time in the beginning to establish some reasonable atmospheres in classes.

"I'd rather have more sycophantism and a lot less ruder-than-Hellism." (a teacher)

Zero Basing: The mildest form of this syndrome is, "I feel like doing something else today." The next layer, "Let's do something different today." "Do we have to work today?" "May we listen to music instead this hour?" "Let's not do anything today." "My 8th grade teacher made this really interesting." (It's not only a repeat but you're deficient to boot. Remember that some teenagers know everything.) Some other types of zero-basing: "This is too hard." "This is too complicated." "I can't do all of that." It gets more vicious and insidious farther up the line with statements from students like, "This class is boring." "I like school except for this class, etc." I call it zero-basing. Let's not do very much "work" today or as little as possible. Let's grind any activity at all to less and less until we have a perfect excuse to say (legitimately) "We never do anything in this class" or "I haven't learned a thing in this class." In other words there is no reason for my having come to school for this classhour and if I can zero-base a couple of additional hours, there's no reason to come to school at all. I would be better off staying at home, going to work, staying over with my boyfriend/girlfriend, etc.

These people are masters at diversionary tactics and are anti-star-fuckers. They're only too glad to tell you what's wrong with you and your class; and they are a constant source of irritation and sometimes depression. They usually are supremely self-confident (at least outwardly), tend to know everything worth knowing already; the world is their oyster. All they have now to do is to have enough time out there to make a mark or a dent or a ripple or perhaps zero-base life, too. They always seem to want to be somewhere they're not at the moment.

$$(2x)^2 = 2x \cdot 2x$$

Most schools seem to try to group students. As faulty as it may be, the following thumbnail descriptions should clarify my use of the terms I've used in categorizing students.

Usually in schools the most highly motivated or personally disciplined students are the college-prep (upper-range) types who can hang in there and see some sort of goal structure at the end of the rainbow, even if it's only to satisfy parental expectations of their "going to college", that panacea of middle-class social and economic aspiration. As long as these kids feel that the program is preparing them for stiffer competition (and their parents reinforce this as these are the very same courses they took 30 years ago) and another and more complicated academic challenge, they'll go along with the system as it exists. They will get restless only if they perceive classes as a waste of time and non-challenging, unenlightening, etc. If the class has bent to zero-basing, they'll tear the roof off, too. This may be another explanation for why the top and bottom student ranges in school have been the most difficult for substitutes.

Schools also have the student who is already a skilled and knowledgeable technician. He's the exception to almost every rule about student behavior. He doesn't have time to misbehave; he doesn't have time for his classmates, either. He is dedicated and expert in one field only. He's the born athlete, the creative wunderkind of costume design, and the electronics wizard at eleven. He is already really good at what interests him, knows where he's going, is practical, knows experts in the field, may already have a mentor. He is a specialist, not a generalist. His major interest is his life, and everything else is quite superfluous. He knows how to read and write and cipher well enough for his taste; so now he wants to get along with his career and *now*, not even next week. School is a bore; typically social contacts are quite limited, except with those who at least pretend initially to have some interest in his chosen field. That other person either joins him and learns something about that specialty or soon they drift apart, and he becomes a loner again. School for this type is a matter of daily survival until he's ultimately liberated.

The middle-rangers are those nice teddy bears, uncomplicated, smiling, average types who just go along, usually uncomplainingly, with whatever they're dealt. They are comfortable to be with because they aren't challenging. Of course, they're the ones who are most frequently neglected. Let the sleeping dogs lie; there are enough problems already.

The low-ender is often a real problem. A lot of the really hard-core and unmotivated will not even stay in high school at all and will make up a disproportionately high percentage of the million drop-outs.

A lot of them didn't learn to read (or at least very well) when they were younger and as lessons tended to get more difficult as they got older, it got really discouraging for many of them. For one group at least they've specialized then in some very practical field that has a very real ending; e.g., they can graduate from high school and know a lot about how to repair a car or do something specific.

They're a challenge in an academic class because they haven't succeeded too well up to now in those, and have often covered their lack of achievement with indifference and/or misbehavior. Often they weren't really occupied by what was going on in that class anyway. Too often teachers have zero-based low-end classes; students suspect that what they're doing has little purpose then and they tear the roof off. Teachers usually dread having these classes; they're not stimulating; they're just challenging. Too frequently these students are shifted off to the newest teacher on campus who is the least prepared of all to deal with them effectively. Low-enders seem to have an uncanny ability to rumple, fold, tear, get greasy and messy any signature card, assignment page, permanent record that they return to you. Be wary of windy days with them.

As a sub your best bet is to try to deal with them firmly but with helpfulness and some warmth. You don't want to alienate them with making the working part of the lesson seem like "assholes and elbows" of military terminology.

My grandmother asked, "How many scholars do you have?" "None, and only a few students" I replied, honestly. They're not your clients either; they're captives. You even have the law on your side.

"Teachers often talk in the big print. Have you ever noticed how raucous a large group of teachers can be?" (a teacher)

"Some students lie even though the truth might serve them better." (a teacher)

"'The reason we study history is to learn from the mistakes of the past.' That's bullshit. No one ever learns anything about history or anything else because each new generation makes its own mistakes, not those of another time and place. That's a lame excuse for learning about that stuff." (a student)

"The same kids who talk knowingly about people snorting cocaine, can also talk knowledgeably about the Peace Corps. They seem so naive in so many ways but superbly sophisticated in others." (a teacher)

'I hated Mrs. Wilson. She had the worst breath of anyone I've every been around." 'I didn't like her either; she was a bitch." (one student to another)

(Student to teacher) 'The thing I like about you; you're so simple." The teacher replied, "Thank you, Susan."

"Teachers who are emotionally and intellectually deficient ought not be teachers." (a student)

And a word from the son of one of my ex-colleagues, "You've got it made now as a substitute, not like my dad who's getting ulcers from teaching."

"Any housewife off the street can be a teacher." (an ex-principal)

"Sixth period I have social science. He is a very nice man; he's cool; his name is Mr. Edwards. I hate social science but he makes it easy and entertaining, and I've really come to enjoy it." (a student)

Do you have any idea how important teachers are to their students? Are you prepared for a kid with straight, black hair who admires his teacher so totally that he tries to reproduce his Afro? Or the kid who breaks a tool that he can't afford to replace and kisses the teacher because the teacher says that "mistakes will happen, and the tool isn't all that important anyway?"

The teacher sets the atmosphere for all kinds of approaches. His attitudes toward scholarship and people are ongoing by the day. The attitudes that are more remote to the school environment and more personal are transmitted in a wide variety of other ways by the teacher. He sets the climate for racial tolerance in the classroom and that can make it especially difficult for the sub. When Scott, from a rural town in Arkansas, said to the black kid in class, "I don't know or care what's in your black heart"; my heart skipped several beats and I was immobilized with uncertainty. There were a lot of things I could have done, so I did and said nothing and that seemed to work. I froze.

If I indicated to Scott that he was a product of some pretty terrible conditioning to hate and fear all of those inferiors out there, I didn't know him well enough to determine whether that sort of statement would mean anything to him at all or simply confuse him and potentially reinforce further his prejudice of (against) inferiors.

With a more enlightened group they would instinctively understand the double edge of the term inferior. Then I wondered how many percentage-wise were *really* enlightened in comparison to that vaster percentage of those not listening at all, half-listening, and the most dangerous of all; those who heard something that I didn't intend to transmit. Simple, concise language is best.

If I made an issue would the black boy be even more humiliated by having some honky taking his side; I didn't know where he was coming from. If I aroused the issue properly there might be a fist-fight (each physically was quite capable of taking care of himself) and that would compound the problem that much further. There would be a winner or loser of that sort of confrontation. So I did nothing except pause for what I hoped was a pregnant time, looked at neither, and then resumed the lesson. It seemed like a terrible responsibility for a sub. I really felt powerless.

On grading a lot of papers one teacher described it

this way: "Students establish patterns. The good ones keep doing good work; the bad ones do badly or do nothing at all. It never changes. Why bother spending a lot of time going over their papers? If you notice some student who is declining or one who is improving, you might read one or two of his things for awhile to see where he's going. Otherwise, you're just wasting your time."

How many teachers are speed readers? I've seen many a teacher using a little technique I call: Grade-a-Glance. Grades go in the grade book about as fast as the papers can be turned over with the other hand. Papers, whole roomsfull, don't take long that way.

"Everybody did so well on the last test, I've got to lower some grades." (a teacher) Why? Aren't you doing something right if so many of your students are accomplishing exactly what you wanted them to? You're the only one who can put a stop to grade escalation (that everybody seems to be concerned about these days), but don't penalize students who are really performing for you. The bell shaped curve is not sacred.

The teacher doesn't give students grades; students 'earn what they deserve' on the work that they have done for that class. If a student questions his grade openly in class and refuses to stop after class to discuss it privately, but insists on your immediate explanation instead, then let him have it publicly. You'll stop that kind of behavior.

Brenot's Irrefutable Laws on Teacher Objectivity and Grading Policy:

1. *The really talented student in art class is most often the one who paints in a style similar to the instructor's, or one the teacher admires especially for its uniqueness.*
2. *In social studies classes, the students well-considered bias which most closely coincides with that of the teacher will get an A in the course.*
3. *In activity classes, only the student who does it well, as well as does it well regularly, and stays well out of the teacher's*

66

Corollary I:

In a writing class the student who writes in the style of the teacher, an author the teacher admires especially, is interested in, or at least writes about things that are of particular interest to the teacher, will do inordinately well in that class.

The Law of Circularity or another vicious circle:

All of this is true except when the teacher is lazy and gives only objective tests. Then he has no idea at all of how his students points of view complement his own. He doesn't get close enough to know them. Then they are graded on their merits; but the tests devised by the teacher, gauge the student's knowledge of the sometimes irrelevant little things the instructor feels are worthy of note after all.

"After *Get Smart* from TV all of those years, one generation thought that chaos was KAOS." (a teacher) If you can still spell after five years of teaching, you've been doing something wrong, or you haven't been reading those papers very zealously. How many other professions have to face "the heroin of the play, while on sumer vacation, went in for diner where she ordered moore of the penut desert."?

The recipe: Bake one frozen pieshell; put in the canned cherry filling and spread ersatz cream topping over the top. That's a recipe? As one parent sarcastically asked his daughter each day, "What kind of cookies did you make today?" Home Ec. (nee cooking classes, more accurately) teachers might consider nutrition as a basis for the lesson of the day, also. One teacher bent and taught her students how to make hamburgers; that threw them off the scent; then she slipped them zucchini quiche, an artichoke sauce for pasta, and spinach stuffed mushrooms. And those were well-thought-through choices nutritionally. There is a genuine problem of home ec. Teachers lack of inspiration in teaching these kids how to cook real foods (they're usually cheaper despite the manufacturer's propaganda — the producers haven't factored in the medical bills). Cooking is not assembling package A with package B and sprinkling package C over the top. It's an art that is also survival.

When you have students with some obvious social or emotional problem, you do what you can to help, or you send them off to their counselor; you do something; you act. If you have a kid in class with a hearing impairment, you move him to a front seat; when you have a student who squints at the board every time there is an assignment, you call his parent or the school nurse (if you still have one) to suggest testing.

If your students have some obvious vitamin deficiency, why not consider advising them on that as well. Remember that most of these problems take a long time to show, so these kids have had those dietary lacks for some time. If someone has a serious lack of concentration, advise brain foods: fish and other seafoods; poor eyesight, eat lots of carrots; for broken nails advise oatmeal and some orange juice for breakfast; milk and other foods rich in vitamin B_2 for hair loss; etc. All of these foods are basic; you're not practicing medicine without a license; not any one of these foods can be too bad for most people.

Please don't laugh *ever* when you assign some kid detention or punish him some way. It's just not an appropriate reaction by an adult, if you didn't know that already.

For oral book reports, try rearranging the seats in a large circle and have the students sit at their own desks to discuss their books. The atmosphere ought to be more encouraging than the traditional up there, knees knocking, terror stricken sessions of old. One type may choose to stand even then.

An alternative assignment might be given that also satisfies those little needs for visible student projects for back-to-school nights, too. Encourage students to make a collage that represents key elements, characters, or situations in their chosen book. (The quality and maturity level of their choices ought to improve also because of having to look for graphic elements.) Have them describe those for the class. One range of student will really appreciate the option.

Even changing the room arrangement has added some non-threatening variety, and that's important to do when a change is relevant.

Ethnic minority girls especially have often been trained to be rather shy and retiring; they're more modest in the shower room, a boisterous girl is really offensive to them, sometimes they won't even look you straight in the eye; they're not being shifty, they just haven't been trained as an Anglo has. Typically, they hate to give oral book reports or oral projects unless they can keep a low profile at their seats. Otherwise, often you find that they have contracted a mysterious disease that will keep them out of school until the heat is off, and you have stopped requiring everyone to give a report up there in front of the rest of the class. They're not going to change; you're going to have to amend the requirement. Some will even appreciate your giving them the option of taping their report which they will ask you to listen to in private. Their rapid recovery will amaze you, medical science, and the attendance office simultanously.

Another way of handling it is to say to the class, "We're running out of time, and there are too many volunteers (or people who have been assigned already). You have the option of turning in a written report if you choose" (and smile gently when you say that). They will produce a finished report, stapled, and in an expensive plastic folder almost like presto-change-o, and they'll thank you eternally for understanding.

Try this technique; it works. Have students write every alternate word of a spelling list (English or foreign language) with their unnatural hand. Since it's such a cumbersome process to form the letters by the opposite hand, they learn to spell better. Now, if you have a whole class of right handers, here's the test: which numbers will be assigned the most difficult words?

If you ever find some real marijuana on campus, just say, "I'll take that home with me and flush it down the toilet there." And if you get away with that, you can send it to me for analysis if you like. (Just testing to see whether you're reading carefully). And that's what a Haydn Surprise is; this has got to be instructive in many ways.

Upper-range students often appreciate assignment sheets; they like to know where the curriculum is taking them. For you it's a good check on content, balance, variety as you must have the right mix of these elements for each section. The low and middling ones don't care whether there's any logical flow in the curriculum; their minds seem to be divided into ten minute attention segments.

If you've done this kind of preplanning, it's easier to find an assignment out of the body of the total, that will be the best one for a substitute day.

If you have scheduled ethnic feast days for foreign language or specialty elective classes, be sure to allow for volunteers first for the clean-up committee. If you have students whose parents are without funds, that assignment will cost them nothing; it's one that must have responsible people. Be sure to make a complete menu (including disposable eating utensils, plates, etc. for the kids who have more money than time) and limit every category with a specified number who may sign up for each.

A male student was scandalized that a female teacher used the term, "faggots". She meant twigs.

"The protagonist got stoned" may sound like a mob throwing rocks to you but to many kids thase days, it may mean that the hero is high on drugs. Similarly, a lid may not be a jar top but 2.2 ounces of grass. A snort when I was a boy was a tipple; today that may be a line.

There are also localisms to contend with. In Ohio, a "raise-in" is the equivalent of a pimple or a zit to a Californian. A raisin is still a dried grape in California. A freeway is a beltway, an expressway, a skyway, a turnpike, a superhighway. To be lame, locally, means that you're stupid or unaware, disorganized, or someone who is personally not altogether. Before class starts at all, put five questions for a math class, a topic sentence for other types, some lines that need to be translated, whatever, on the board. The kids have exactly five minutes to complete the assignment (you might want to use a timer with a bell for this). Meanwhile, you take roll. When the bell rings, you collect the papers. These must be graded and recorded if you don't do any other papers all year.

Around Halloween there can be a spate of crank phone calls, threats to egg your house or to damage your car, or some other equally petty but harassing behavior. It's mostly talk and a device to see how you'll react; if you don't react visibly, it will stop usually. If for some reason a student "has it in for you" something relatively minor may happen at this time. Except for politicians (whose critics are too frequently deadly serious), businessmen in recent years, and actors, few other occupational groups put up with a threatening public. You can always resort to an unlisted phone.

"Have a good weekend, a pleasant afternoon, a joyous holiday" is not said automatically and universally by all teachers. Some don't say anything; they have shitty manners personally (that's a Haydn Surprise for you); they have never been trained to think about the comfort and safety of someone else, much less a whole classroom full of people they really don't want to get close to. Students need to be told to *always, everyday, every classhour* by their teacher who must say at the end of the period, "Have a really pleasant day." Everyone is buoyed; and it's so easy to say, once you get the hang of it.

In education a lot of time seems to be spent in going over what you might have thought was obvious, especially since you already know it yourself. If you've said it once, you must have said it a couple of times before if you've been teaching for any length of time. There is a tendency sometimes to skip over some vital and logical steps in the expositions that are necessary to make the topic intelligible. It's all new information to someone out there. Another problem for teachers is that in reaching back for common threads to weave together so that all students are together, they go back too far and bore everyone to death with too much repetition. It's really hard to do a step-by-step, fool-proof sequence explaining how to do it, select it, create it.

Sometimes, teachers select the wrong words to explain the lesson and students miss the point entirely. Example;

71

The girl entered the school in the blue dress. What needs to be said here is, "How many of you have seen a school wearing a blue dress?" "The prepositional phrase goes right next to the word it modifies."

Students don't seem to want to be singled out publicly either for negative (trouble) or positive accomplishments (the resut of a job well-done). They seem to prefer relative anonymity and your quiet and personal encouragement instead. The exception to this that I've noticed is that if there's tracking and they are totally with their own, they feel very comfortable with praise.

One teacher had created such a complicated point system for various kinds of assignments that he tended to assign fewer and fewer projects for students to do. He ran out of time to grade, record, and make corrections and comments on the students' papers.

Students seem to want to hear about the teacher's experiences at the time when he was the same age. It's a reassurance, I think, that the student will accomplish at least as much as the teacher. He wants to know that the teacher was a regular fellow and not a hybrid. It's another way of relating.

If you run into a really boring section in the curriculum, compress it drastically, explain that it is a necessary bridge to the next step. Students will accept that. If you find that a couple of years worth of students tune out on a particular area of your course, amend it or scrap it entirely. It must not be doing what you thought it would. Don't hang on to it as if it were a sacred object. Try not to save these little nuggets for sub days also. A sub can spot a throwaway lesson instinctively. So can students, and they react accordingly. The momentum of the course can go ahead (more slowly than when the teacher is there, however) if the lesson is properly structured to conform to the basic rules of the format.

In any class, when it takes 15 minutes to finish roll (often because the teacher hasn't laid down the law about lateness) or the teacher fiddles and stalls away time unnecessarily, allows too much time for students to accomplish very little, that class has too much dead time. The class will get rowdy and difficult to get back for classtime instruction when the instructor finally does get himself pulled together.

Dead time increases to zero basing. If you accelerate your program gradually, you'll be amazed at how much students can do in addition to your basic program and will actually like school better because they are learning more and getting a better sense of accomplishment. Don't gallop them every day; leave some room for your warm relationship too.

Social adjustment seems to happen inevitably as the person matures. His primary reason for being in school at all is for learning something.

What activity shall we do today? Give the students the choice of a) the spelling review, b) the literature lesson, c) the grammar exercise; e.g., a very limited number of options but the things you want to accomplish in the next day or two. You allow the students to share in the decision process and everything gets done eventually anyway.

Another technique for creating the illusion of student choice is to give them options 1, 2, and 3 of the date when a major paper is due. Make one choice a Monday, another that Friday, and the other the following Friday. Curiously, classes don't always choose the last date suggested. Once the deadline is established reasonably and rationally and by majority vote, don't change it for anything.

Some students, and especially the zero basers, will say some really hurtful things now and then. Probably your best defense is to smile and thank them for their thoughtfulness, or generosity, or regard, or concern. You might even confront them by asking what their motive was for saying what they did. Do remember that they are still learning the boundaries of acceptable approaches; you do have to build some ego armor, however, for survival; but you don't have to organize a Sicilian-style vendetta and beat them bloody for every transgression.

Teenagers take themselves very seriously. Anything they perceive of as a put-down is grist for a long-standing resentment which can be very damaging (to buildings and grounds as well) unless you consciously try to counteract it. Be generous and forgiving, and you might find on closer contact that this kid really likes you now that you're not just another anonymous authority figure. A lot of negativism seems to come from the uninvolved. They won't join you until you create a comfortable atmosphere especially for them, or another activity that they can relate to. And maybe just talking to one nice adult is all that is needed for a limited breakthrough.

One teacher holds a personal detention for a single student after school. The kid is given some minor job to do like cleaning the blackboard and they chat. So many kids seem to need closer contact with someone they feel is reasonable and who likes them. All too often the student will open up about something that's going wrong at home. This is a one on one session; allow students who need academic help to join you and that adds another validity; don't allow two behavior problems to be with you on the same day, however.

You might consider a differentiation between a child who breaks a school rule and is sent off to administrative detention, and one who misbehaves in your class; he's your problem, and you take care of it.

A technique left over from the positive thinking school of manipulation usually will work with a student you absolutely detest for some reason. You find one thing about this inferior slob that you genuinely can admire: an obviously new dress, a hairstyle that was well-done and complementary. Tell them how much you like it. They will be startled at first and a little hesitant, but will be your admirer from then on.

Don't hesitate to tell the kid who specializes in auto shop that you wish you had taken an auto repair class yourself. He'll appreciate your respect for his interest and talent.

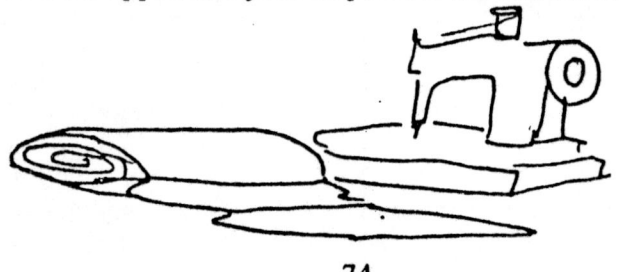

74

Brenot's Variable and Non-Immutable Law of
Teacher Abstinence: Teachers generally are
divided into three groups — those who drink
too much during school and those who drink
to much after school. The rest are teetotalers.

To the Substitute:

After you've been on campus a few times, you'll have
students from prior classes. They like to see a familiar face
and will help you a great deal to put pressure on any classmates who resist if they grew to like you before.

"Hi, Lola Ferragamo!" "How do you know that?"
"I subbed for your sewing class." "You remembered my
name?" "You bet!"

You bet indeed. This was the con-artist; I'm getting
out of this classroom this hour and am going to do something different. Try wheedling after that declaration before
you become indignant, but become outraged after the
whining. What an act! If this kind of thing goes on too long,
turn away and get busy doing something else or start talking
to someone else or start talking to someone else. It will go
on endlessly until you do.

Each hour that you're on campus, try to memorize at
least four names. Use any associative technique — fear is a
starter. Then you can elaborate after that. You'll be surprised how fast those add up over weeks and any aid to control is welcome. Every kid likes to be known and recognized
so you make a lot of points also.

Remember that the regular teacher has the luxury of
a week or two to learn his students' names. But he *must*
learn them within that time for control and to establish a
love/trust relationship. He has accurate roll sheets; he can
arrange his classroom any way he wants (or rearrange, if that
perception of his students is not right or accurate after all);
he can place his students in any patterning that suits his
fancy this season. Usually everyone learns 1) the harder to
control troublemaker first, then 2) the names of the very best
students in the class; then 3) gradually fills in with the
middling ones who don't give him, or anyone else, much

trouble anyway. Except for a confusing pocket of Debbies and Marks which may take a little longer, everyone is identified within the first week or two.

As a sub you don't have that luxury. Often you've got the five minutes between classes for an initial assessment and about five minutes maximum into the classhour to learn the names of one or two potential detractors and settle them down so that you can get on with it. The anxiety level increases proportionally as you have fewer things to help you, like seating charts. But if everything else fails, don't take a pill, take a poll.

A minor point, really, but one more aspect of reversing the long-standing, anti-sub campaign. Print you name, somewhere on your accounting of the day left for the regular teacher. And rather than being referred to anonymously as "the sub", you gain validity if the teacher refers to you by name instead.

You must insist on the right to assign detention. It's power and that's control, too.

When I reported on the capsule of the day sheet that one little freshman's behavior was unacceptably infantile, his teacher couldn't quite accept the idea that he should punish him on someone else's advice. And so the freshman was told that if there was another bad report, his detention time would be tripled. My heart jumped when I heard that one. I thought that according to my analysis I wouldn't be able to sub for that teacher again. He had unknowingly destroyed my power base and that would also work against me in other classes where those same students would be. I tried another day. The girl across the aisle spent the whole classtime baiting and bothering that kid to see just how much it would take to get him busted. I ignored her; why reinforce that? It was a really unpleasant kind of atmosphere which could have been avoided easily. When I was talking this problem over with my wife, voila! She came up with an answer that was not only simple and direct, but downright brilliant. Ask the principal if he had any objection to my assigning detention on my own. He didn't. Quite the reverse. I did it sparingly and students said, "Can a sub do that?" "I'm not going to go; it isn't fair." I explained calmly that for any time not served it was doubled each day to a 4 hour maximum when the student was suspended.

If, on the detention slip, you put: 1) your name in block letters FOR 2) regular teacher's last name, you establish yourself as an entity and you imply to the student that the regular teacher would have punished the transgressor similarly if only he had been there.

If you can't handle anymore and you're kicking the kid out of class now, don't slap the slip down unless your ego absolutely demands it. It's better to walk over to the kid, hand him the slip, with a gesture of your thumb, say "Out!", or say simply, "Pick up your slip on your way out of class." Now don't get into a direct confrontation or a verbal exchange. Go back to the front. If the kid takes an interminable time to get his body out of there, lean against the desk (jellyfish) and wait. In any direct confrontation the sub will lose. He's not really a member of the family and those members will come to the defense of a threatened one.

Don't ever give a student a second chance. There really aren't many of those. After Shh; quiet, please; hush; QUIET, it's a 10th chance, not a second one. Don't be that forgiving; it's often perceived as weakness, not flexibility and generosity. After you put on the board, "talking = Detention" and a student's name and your warning goes unheeded, assign detention (quietly and without anger). They got out of bounds and they have to pay the price. It is their problem, not yours. I'm not your warden; I'm your surrogate teacher. Don't use any more muscle than the occasion absolutely demands. Don't overkill. Save the really loud bellow for the time when needed only. Be firm but pleasant. Expect reasonable student behavior (and do something fast if it isn't) and more and more frequently, you'll get it.

You have a talkative and outwardly defiant student on your hands. What do you do? If you say, "Move your seat and move there." (You point it out with your finger, specifically), inevitably, most of that type of student will try to sit somewhere other than where you indicated. This is a *major test*; it's not as casual as you might think. This is your reputation on the line as a "hard-ass type" (in Army terms: "Someone who ain't going to take no shit from nobody") who follows through on every little thing in class. It may be worth it to you in the long run to demand and be somewhat petty in the beginning. It's easier to be more like yourself later if the class is firmly controlled from the start. But then don't make this student the class model; try to isolate him instead and neutralize him. Let him be the odd-man-out; let him sulk, turn and say something amusing and smile. Break the tension for the rest of the class. If he later comes around, welcome him back.

On the day before a major holiday break, expect the worst. The kids are anticipating turkeys, sugar plums, and Easter rabbits and the warmth and comfort of those holidays. School is not where they want to be. Only the kids who are mistreated at home or have few warm family connections will dread holidays.

Be sure to note that there are a lot of gradations of misbehavior. Some kid who gets out of his seat to sharpen a pencil has done nothing wrong (if that's all he actually does), but the student who disappears right after roll has. Bust him for that and next time you're on campus, it will be that much easier. Don't abuse the detention privilege yourself by being too petty after you've established yourself as an entity on campus. A lot of detention is tokenism anyway; for a first offense, 15 minutes is enough. It's a gentle reminder to the student that there are some standards.

Don't be totally restrictive; I've found it better to be more flexible, personally. Students love to try to hit the wastebasket from their seats. If they do miss give them a thumbs down and a high-sign that they are to pick up the miss. If they, however, hit it, clap or give them a thumbs up. It's just a small way of becoming somewhat human in their eyes and that's important, too. If shooting for the basket bothers you, try this approach. You hold the basket and tell the student that if he misses, he has to clean up any paper on the floor. When he shoots, you move the basket; everyone laughs; the kid has gotten the attention that he needed; and you then circulate with the basket and ask students to pick up any mess on the floor. It works out nicely this way, too.

What if the lesson sent is, "Have students read chapter 8 and answer questions 1, 3, 5, 7, 8, and 9 in detail. Please collect at the end of the hour"? Ideal lesson type, right?

Yes, but what if a spokesman or two from the class say, "But what if we don't?" Then you must say, "If anyone chooses not to do the assignment sent by your teacher, each will take the consequence." (not "you will pay the consequences", as that's potentially plural again and some possibility of safety in numbers). Repeat the assignment verbally and whatever you do maintain vocal and body language calm (if possible, try to look even more relaxed plysically as you add a slight crispness and edge to your voice; you're more threatening this way).

Now you absolutely must be honest with your capsule of the day sheet. If you have a name or two of the instigators, advise the teacher. If not, describe the confrontation fully (and often the instructor will be able to guess who the primary troublemakers will have been). Their papers may be missing. Ask him to assign some sort of appropriate punishment. There must be some sort of consequence or penalty. Ask him to prepare his classes differently for future sub days. If he's not willing to bestir himself to make his classes manageable, refuse to sub for him again. If no one is willing to cover his classes, either an administrator or a fellow colleague will have to face his unruly broods, and pressure from on high or shame will eventually bring him around.

Don't hesitate to amend the *format* of the lesson to conform to what you know will work better for a sub. Add compulsion, a time deadline, your "helping", etc. if those elements are missing. However, do not change the lesson's *content*. A film of Damon Runyon's story "The Gift of the Magi" to be shown the day or so before Christmas vacation and for students to write a descriptive essay about, does not mean that the sub can show "The Tin Mines of Bolivia" with the same effect; especially if the writing assignment doesn't key into the general themes being developed in the curriculum. And that happens too frequently. What teacher hasn't complained that good lessons have been destroyed by poor subs and, therefore, they have resorted to a maintenance dose that fakes the day until they get back?

Don't be guilty of having lost some valuable lesson keys (time consuming to redo), of having scrambled lessons intended for other classes, of having generally screwed-up everything that day. Stick as closely as possible to the script and everyone will be happier. *The Gift of the Magi* film after the holidays will have lost much or all of its timeliness and impact and what teacher will thank you for ruining a really valid lesson?

Amend the lesson sent to conform to what you know about the absolute necessity of *completion*. If an emergency lesson says, "Read the next chapter and answer the questions at the end of the chapter.", do a fast scan and either divide the assignment for so much to be done in class with the remainder as homework. Or announce that all work completed by the end of the hour (at their own pace) should be turned in with any not completed to receive reduced credit the following day. In other words, you must add some compulsion, rewards, and negatives.

Also, don't hesitate to amend the *style of presentation*. For my "introduce fractions" debacle, the teacher had noted in caps and underlined *DO NOT GIVE STUDENTS WORK-SHEETS UNTIL THEY HAVE HAD THE INTRODUCTION.* Why, I have no idea. I tried it her way once and it didn't work. I turned my back to the class, started her elaborate diagram scheme, perhaps said a couple of words in explanation before the paper balls began bouncing back and forth. The next classhour I did it my way, gave them the ditto sheets on which they had to put their names. I stood squarely in front of them and explained how to look at and solve sample problem 1. Each kid had to put his head down and concentrate on the explanation because there were 9 more problems in that series that depended on his understanding. Then I went to number 10, 20, etc. As the atmosphere relaxed, I wandered down the aisles and helped individually. That way worked for me.

If the teacher has said, "Have students do work sheet, give answers and have study for exam next week.", you're in real trouble if you do that. Remember, most regular teachers have never substituted or did it a long time ago and have forgotten. You must turn this instructive lesson into an exam to add the right note of *compulsion*. Trade papers, put your name at the bottom of the one you're grading (any "errors" in grading will be deducted from the score of the person who made the mistake), put the number right or wrong in a circle at the top. It must be turned in to you at its completion, even if the regular teacher does no more than give it the weight of a 1-10 scale or√+,√ , and √-. That must be done for every assignment while a sub is on campus. If the teacher fails to do this, you're in trouble the next time. However, you do still have alternate power with detention, star-fuck, grading potential next time, etc. It's not all lost on a single issue; the more the better though, obviously.

If you see that the lesson is too short, lengthen it. Why not do it first rather than last and legitimately run out of time. You've finished roll and it's time for your monologue. The reason your teacher isn't here today? Well, my dears, listen to this line of malarky. You can easily spin it out to 5-10 minutes depending on inspiration, the cooperation of the old silver tongue and those little dears out there.

Even after the lesson has begun the regular teacher has the option of shifting emphasis in mid-stream if he sees that its format isn't working as planned or anticipated. There will be a grumbling but he can convert it to a quiz to be graded in so many minutes if necessary. You can't do that as a sub. The lesson, once started, is more static. You must be positive and know exactly where you're going and any transgression of that is weakness. Think through your instructions to the class carefully beforehand, and say it right the first time. Amend the lesson so that is conforms *as closely as possible* to what you know is optimal or necessary for control. Then juggle that around so that you come *as closely as possible* to the intent of the teacher.

The substitute had had unruly classes all day; the floor was awash with paper, desks were overturned; gum had been shot with rubber-band slingshots at the ceiling and clung there in globs; the desks were coated with writing. During the classhour the sub sent for some spray cans of cleaner and cloths or a roll of paper towels so at least all of the decorative graffiti could be eradicated. Two spray bottles were delivered; she handed them to the chief behavior problems in that class; and guess what happened next? The two boys sprayed one another and then their classmates and that class hour was even worse, if that's possible by definition, bedlam as well. Screaming reached an even more frantic pitch.

What should the sub have done instead? The sub should have handed the cloth or roll of towels to a little goody-two-shoes type. Then she should have circulated around the classroom and sprayed the desks that needed cleaning. The miscreants should have received detention. She should *not* have let such an attractive weapon get out of her control.

This was the lesson left for two afternoon freshman world history classes. Before we began I was instructed to read: "Students are to complete a two-page textbook test as a worksheet (in 15-20 minutes). They started it yesterday in class and are to keep it overnight and use it as a study sheet for tomorrow's test. Give them the correct answers. Then show them the film *The Aegean World*."

If I told them all of the answers there wouldn't be any reason at all for students to waste time and do the assignment for themselves. It might be better to talk with all of their friends and wait for the correct answers to be given. As long as they knew the material in time for tomorrow's *test* which *counts*, the rest of this was irrelevant. Their thirst for knowledge would have dried up instantly. This exercise had to be a test too. In 15 minutes papers were to be completed, exchanged with a neighbor who would put his name at the bottom of the sheet, answers given, a tally of incorrect circled at the top, and returned to the owner for review and any discussion or clarification.

If a student ever asks if the papers are to be collected, *always* say yes. When that time comes, say, "Save those papers and turn them in tomorrow. You might want to review that sheet for the test tomorrow," or "Remember the test tomorrow" is a little less transparent.

There are few things more pitiful than an adult who thinks that he is putting something over on a teenager. Inevitably, some kid will see through the whole thing. Deny anything; it looks like potential chance anyway, and that's enough. This gets more difficult if the teacher has multiples of the same course during the day. If that happens, simply shift the order of activity so that the review sheet does come last and you do really run out of time. The ending is a breathless photo finish. Then, "Please keep your paper until tomorrow and turn it in with your test paper." Sometimes the timing is tricky because you've got to manipulate the language so that it can be easily misunderstood. You don't

really need to lie; you just arrange and rearrange your statements so that they work better for you. It's creative phraseology. So many people seem to hear only what they want to
anyway. And that's selective hearing.

This sort of manipulative scheme could become less
frequent as administration and teachers become more aware
of what is needed for substitute days.

*Brenot's next-to-last comment on teaching
salaries: Any teacher who's currently paid
what he's worth should be fired. This means
that:*

a)   All teachers are underpaid.
*b)   The school ought to hire aides, or less ex-
      pensive teachers and fire the expensive
      ones.*
c)   You must fire those not doing a good job.
*d)   All of the above because your answer de-
      pends on your interpretation, point of
      view, orientation, learning style.*

*I wrote this question thinking that everyone
would automatically understand that I felt that
teachers were hopelessly underpaid and under-
appreciated. Answer (a) would have been my
right answer but there were several more inter-
pretations and correct answers to my test —
and some of yours?*

As a sub, if you need something done for you in class,
always choose a little cypher, a mouse, a goody-two-shoes
type. They're reliable and can follow directions.

Students tend to be conservative (down-right reac-
tionary) and want everything done as it always is, no devia-
tion allowed. An unwanted and complained-of reading time
is sorely missed on the day when it's purposely forgotten.

As a sub, run your own A-V equipment. There's nothing like some smart-ass volunteer who slows down the speed, breaks the film, gets it slightly out of focus, turns the volume up and down just enough one way or the other to make the experience irritating instead of instructive. If the teacher has designated some responsible type, try him out; but take over if he missteps once. He may be a star-fucker. You avoid even the potential hazard by doing it yourself. If you see lack of attention or talking, don't hesitate to speak up once, freeze frame the film, or turn off the machine entirely and wait. The comfort of some A-V piece running is jarred and pressure will be applied by the others on any talkers.

Introduce all films. Even if the title is ambiguous and you have to stop it a couple of minutes after the title and credits, do it. Put it into some sort of reference or framework. Many students today, as an adjunct of the entertain-me-generation, are visual illiterates. They have seen so much television and so many movies that media is not instructive unless you help them see themes or specific bits of information. A-V doesn't teach itself. Make some sort of assignment. "List the major points made in the film" is a good hedge against non-preview — and, of course, this is to be turned in at the end of the hour. It must be "counted". Or make a quiz on the film as Plan B (number 1-10) and do it.

During a longer or especially bad movie, go to the front of the room periodically. Do something like looking slowly through papers on the lectern and glance at the film now and then, take a tall stool and slowly move it over to the side of the room (usually nearest the door) and watch part of the film from there. Do everything very slowly. Stretch your legs out like a lounging riverboatman in a George Caleb Bingham picture or hunch over like Rodin's *Thinker*. Stay non-threatening. You only react more harshly if absolutely necessary as a result of some rude behavior. The fact also that you're visibly watching the film gives it more importance and that is an additional control factor.

Do the sub a favor category. Bad films are terrible. The current topic of the class was the Civil War and Reconstruction; however, the lesson for this last day before Christmas vacation was to show a film called, "The Declaration of Independence, Part 1" or as an alternate, "Daniel Boone", in either case a nice bit of continuity for the course. The production had been done on the cheap and so ludicrous and phony that it can best be described as pure kitsch. If you tried to take it seriously yourself as a model for students, your credibility could only drop to minus zero. I made the mistake of asking my all-purpose "list the major points" questions. At the hands of the more acute students these were hilarious as there were no points at all. If this had been a low-range group, the results would not have been amusing.

The second part of a lesson was to show a movie, "The Aegean World". The tourists wandering around the archeological sites being described were all dressed in early 1950's fashions, and were uniformly old themselves. And if piles of rocks (ruins) and wrinkles closely coincide, it seems harder to empathize. The film didn't have any core or cohesion; it had nothing to say, and it kept saying it.

I was certainly glad that we had lived and taught in Greece and had visited the places being described. I stopped the film, tried to give them some personal view of what was being shown, fill in some of the gaps, describe the newer theory of the immolation of Santorini. The film had done its dirty work; they just had been programmed out again. I was really sorry. For the second class, I turned the sound off and simply narrated it. It went much better that way and the questions and discussion carried on after the visual part was finished. Incidentally, I did the narration from the front of the room and that much eye contact seemed to help enormously.

If you get slipped a really odious example of off-Hollywood amateur hour, try turning off the sound, giving it your own humorous dialogue. It's better not to dignify some of those films by even pretending to take them seriously. Tell the students (and you note also on your capsule of the day sheet) to advise the teacher to consider taking that film off his list of usable ones.

Some students don't want to be at school at all, but if they are required to be there, they don't want their time wasted by an emotional spree. Incidentally, some students genuinely look forward to the social contacts, the academic challenges, the good feelings of being in a nice, secure setting. A bad substitute day can be disaster for that kind of student also. So do it right.

"May we leave early? This is boring." "I was excused to go to the library for the rest of the week as all of my regular work is completed." "I'm on independent study." "I'm the aide." "We have to get ready for the assembly next hour.", etc.

Learn to be hard-nosed, believe no one — because the kid who gets excused will be the one who shouldn't have been let out of solitary confinement (much less a classroom), and he'll be the one who will blame you for something to either divert attention or accuse you of not controlling him properly.

Bathroom excuse can be a real problem for subs. One teacher used a sign-in/out sheet with good effect as that tended to intimidate massive numbers from leaving the classroom. Unless there is a really obvious emergency, let only one student at a time leave; tell him that there is a five minute maximum, that no other student may leave until his return. It adds just enough pressure. And they usually come back right away.

Watch the request by counselor slips carefully. If it doesn't say immediately, and if it's at your convenience, let them leave when you've finished with the most important thing being done that classhour. Otherwise, they're going to be concerned with that primarily and get virtually nothing accomplished anyway. It's amazing how threatening a summons from the office is for most kids. They seem to assume that it is always bad news. It's like a telegram in the night to a lot of students.

Don't look at your watch or clock so that students can see you do it. Always go behind them to gauge the time; otherwise, they'll get restless immediately. Know when the class hour is *officially* over, not when the students tell you it is. It's standard to try to get outr of class early. It's the last chance to put something over on you that classhour. And even the best class will try. The end of the classhour is the students' last chance of doing something different as a result of having a sub. The inevitable question is: "May we leave early?" if the lesson isn't long enough or is paced improperly. All administrations are hung-up on keeping all students in the classroom until the bell actually rings, as the snowball effect school-wide can be devastating. The more controlled teacher then becomes the bad guy, and that's totally unfair.

When students stand and stretch, walk to the door, fast, because the next move is going to be toward the door and out the door. It's inevitable. If necessary, hold the door handle behind you; don't worry, they're not going to trample you. You may lose a couple of kids out a side door; but don't worry, you've controlled and contained the bulk. Smile and wish as many as possible a pleasant day as you need to re-establish your calm self after having lost control at this last gasp. It's important for the next time you're on campus. If there is not a door, establish a magic line with your body (stretch your arms out if necessary), don't stand across the room from the opening and expect students to be controlled verbally. Keep the classroom door closed, generally. You invite fewer distractions that way. At one school without doors at all, the teachers back was to the corridor (not the students backs to the door). That's even worse for the substitute.

"Today we had a stuck-up old lady as a sub in science, so Mark unplugged the big fish aquarium. I thought that he was going to leave it unplugged, but he didn't. Tomorrow Debbie, Kelley, and I are going to bring a cup of coffee and put it in the fish aquarium." (Student Journal entry)

You're not from a lower range group yourself, otherwise you wouldn't be a teacher or a sub by definition. Sometimes it's hard for you to relate to where a student is coming from. Is senseless vandalism the product of a lack of feeling associated, retaliation for some slight, boredom, or what? Has anyone done a study on that problem? If the contentious atmosphere of schools, staff and policy choices are causing their own problems, then we're in real trouble. That's three kids who would be willing to kill a whole tank of fish to show that "stuck-up old lady."

Use music to soothe and calm. Keep the volume low so that very much noise makes it impossible to hear, or you turn it off entirely if it gets too noisy. Choose something mellow, no punk-rock cacophony. Know the music that is to be played. You don't need Pink Floyd blaring "We don't need no education" or Jim Morrison "Squirming like a Toad". Don't try to play it safe by choosing the last century's greatest hits as played by the thousand and one strings and woodwind ensemble. That kind of music may be okay for lulling the patrons of supermarkets and department stores but many students don't like the sound. They prefer original groups, not selections from the works of. You can still get away with Simon and Garfunkel and the Beatles stuff today. It's so familiar that even "Rocky Raccoon" is old family.

The best way to get students to participate in a Stop and Read program is for you to do that yourself. Stop and Read, for those unfamiliar with it, is a 10 minute period, usually in the morning when everyone is fresh, when the whole school stops dead in its tracks and everyone reads: groundsmen, principal, switchboard operator. Let the phones ring; they'll call back. Ask the community to join you and perhaps Johnnie will learn to read a bit later but after all. If you're having trouble getting students to get involved at the beginning of the program, read a serialized or segmented story to them each day. Something like an Agatha Christie mystery ought to be right for most groups. Before the one who done it is revealed, stop and have the students write their own endings and solution. Then read them her ending. One book read together ought to be enough. Then encourage them to bring something of their own choice. Often they'll bring another Agatha Christie if they enjoyed the first one. Try *Ten Little Indians* or *N or M*. This is one of *the* three exceptions to reading yourself in front of the students (Test and course materials are okay and if you read to them.) Don't grade papers, make phone calls, or do anything but spend that time reading along with the class. The most frustrating part once you've gotten into it, is to stop. Your natural inclination will be to spend the rest of the classhour engrossed in your selection. Play by the rules, however. If a student tries to interrupt you, say "This is reading time; I'll be able to talk to you in a few minutes." In other words, make the act of reading a sacred event. Incidentally, there is no reason on this earth that you should feel compelled to censure someone else's reading taste. If the kid chooses comic books, porn, the race car driver's manual, a catalogue, whatever, is of no concern of yours. He's reading, and that's what that program is all about.

Sometimes you must develop selective hearing. If some kid comes on with a Hell or Damn by mistake, rather than making an issue of the term, simply don't hear it. It's not a major crime unless you make it one. To err is human. If some little goody-two-shoes type then says, "Did you hear what he said?" you say, "No, dear, what did he say?". She'll purse her lips but will not repeat it. Isn't that nice? If it doesn't exist, don't create it. "Shit" "I wouldn't have in my hand what you've had in your mouth." Curiously, this dictum from my algebra teacher still works today. If some little wise-ass freshman then chimes in, simply say, "We've got to be more careful and keep our act clean." You've reestablished the standard and everyone will be happy. Don't assign detention or any other punishment. Drop it.

When I think of some of the foolish standards my mother, may her soul rest in peace, laid on us as kids, my two sisters and I, I'm surprised we survived the burden of all that perfection. She didn't teach us to swear, believe me; we learned that elsewhere instead, in school as I recall. We had admonition superimposed over so many thou shalt nots, nice people do this or that, this way, if they know any better, those who know the acceptable way, are refined, have been trained to do or say this or that this way and only that way so help me God. It's nice to be an adult and rid of a lot of that. If someone comes to tell you that he is the grand nephew of the reigning vizier, at the court of where-ever, just say, "I won't tell anyone if you won't". That usually stops them. Wha thet's another one of them Haydn Surprises in itself, now ain't it? And that's one of those standards that I've reassessed. I was trained as a child to believe that there were inherent differences between us refined, knowledgeable, sophisticated and worldly urban dwellers and those unrefined, stupid and ignorant, rude clods, and boorish oafs to boot who were rural folks. What incredible and childish values my mother sometimes trained us in. I'm glad to have lived long enough for the time to undo some of that kind of foolishness with our own children and with students. I wonder if there's a reverse stereotype among rural families? (Something about city slickers?) It's like the westerner's perception of the eastern establishment type as a stuffy, unthinking traditionalist. A grey suit does not an intellect or gentleman make, just as a pair of Levis can't create a cowboy. We seem to have developed some interesting ways to pull ourselves apart as a nation.

For real emergencies carry your own bag of tricks in the trunk of your car. A book of really fascinating short stories (geared hopefully to a range of age and interest) is good, lessons from mythology; try some of Thurber's moral tale updates like "The Little Girl and the Wolf", "The Tiger Who Would Be King", "The Princess and the Tin Box" or use "The Secret Life of Walter Mitty", or "The Catbird Seat" as departure points for writing assignments or discussion. (Students love to be read to.) Try some slides of a place you enjoyed visiting, resorts, or places of historical interest seem to be best for this; try word games; or, try an article reproduced that you can distribute, have read, and questions written. Anthropology and sociology are safe topics, especially if you can find one which presents a logical argument. It's useable for almost any class then. Find examples of moral paradoxes from *Values Clarification* or *Choices, Situations To Stimulate Thought and Expression* and structure these for discussion or a written assignment.

Reproduce the Smithsonian Magazine article, *Go West Young Man and Stay Healthy* March 1983. Of all of the publications in America, if you must choose only one, subscribe to the Smithsonian; it's endlessly stimulating and entertaining.

What if there's "nothing to do particularly" that last 10 minutes of class? Use a filler. What if a counselor has come to your class that hour, but leaves you with seven minutes left as he glides out the door, or there is a two minute hiatus between the special bulletin read over the loudspeaker and the bell? There are a lot of ways to supply a needed filler for any dead time at the end of a classhour, too. Those leave awkward times that VPs, directors of activities, and counselors seem to be unaware of. And they say they don't want you to let your classes out early? It's kind of inconsistent, isn't it?

The classroom teacher can't use the same format each day; there must be variety; so depend on some less than optimal days now and then. He's always had success presenting a particular lesson this way. The teacher takes some leverage, constraints, power, and options for granted and doesn't realize that you need those same ones to make the lesson work for you as it would for him. Nothing is always perfect, however. Roll with some punches.

So don't tell the teacher that everything went simply wonderfully, when the reality was that students were bouncing off the walls and hanging from the chandeliers. The teacher won't be able to back you for something that didn't happen. With unfavorable reports from students and neighboring teachers, you then become an incompetent liar. Be honest instead, and tell it like it was.

This has been a long-standing problem and misunderstanding. If it's to be corrected or even improved, your report must be accurate. Don't blame everything on the lesson format. If you goofed up the timing, or classroom management, or presented the lesson badly yourself, don't try to pin everything on a faulty lesson. Learn from your own errors and make adjustments accordingly. Next time should be better.

The sub actually said to the class, "This film is dumb; and I don't know why you're being shown it. I still don't know what it's all about." It was about *Impressionism*. Now any adult who is the graduate of an institution of higher learning ought to be ashamed of not knowing at least something about impressionism. If the sub is deficient, nothing can make a success of the best structured lesson.

The regular teacher had a high absentee rate and was finally asked to take the rest of the year off. The students had for the next six weeks a different sub almost daily. There was, of course, runaway misbehavior. The sub I talked with had been hired for most of the second semester. "How did you finally settle the classes down, and how long did it take?" "We became buddies; and it took to the end of the year actually". . ."The classes were geography and since I had traveled extensively, one day per week I showed slides. They would comment on my being too fat as I was riding the camel, or looking windblown at the Great Wall, and we established a nice relationship."

First, buddies is wrong. If she had only become loving parent instead and interested in their welfare, comfort, and protection rather than her own ego and appearance, those kids would have welcomed her especially after the disorder of so many weeks.

Take roll in pencil and use the standardized absence and tardy symbols for that school. The teacher has enough extra stuff to do on his return and doesn't have time to correct your work, too.

Put all materials back where you found them. Tell the teacher on your daily report sheet where completed papers were put. Don't scatter.

Try not to confront a student openly. If you want to threaten him with decapitation or castration, do it privately and quietly. You want shock value, not a screaming session in an open forum. You're the outsider; so if there's any choice at all; the regular class member, if threatened openly, will always be right.

If you see a flaw on a student's paper, tell him about it quietly and privately also. His error is not a matter of life and death and doesn't need to be made into an object lesson for the ages. Be kindly and helpful instead.

The power of positive thinking may have fallen on hard times in some quarters recently. However, there seems to be a high correlation between an adult's optimism and enthusiasm for something and that atmosphere transmitted to the next generation as a happy and nice thing also. Keep it appropriate, however. It's one thing to feel wonderful about the birth of a child, but you don't have to jump up and down, clap your hands, and squeal with glee, universally love and adore *everything*. Some things are relatively good, better, and best; and vive la difference! Totally unselective adults just seem foolish.

Be honest enough to admit that the subject area of a class is not your specialization. That implies a range of co-operation among you all working together to get the lesson done. It doesn't take long anyway for you to reveal your ignorance and weakness in the subject.

As a sub, don't criticize teachers. They get enough of it from zero-basers and periodically from the administration. They also get a liberal dosage of criticism from the community which tends to blame every flaw of the new generation on the failure of public education to be all things to everyone and/or correct every social ill that may come along.

At the end of the classhour with less than 10 minutes, set up a contract. Say, "We can't possibly finish all of that. I'll go around and check to see that everyone is doing as well as he can; and I'll write a note to your instructor and tell him that I have allowed you the extra time to finish it tonight at home. For any who aren't working industriously, extra time will not be given." Go slowly so that your appraisal takes the whole time left.

Postulate:
If the basic teacher has terrible control or has created a contentious atmosphere in the class, the job of just controlling the class will be that much more difficult for the sub.

Maintain vocal calm: Don't shriek or screech, bellow instead if it's desperate. Lower your pitch; don't raise it. Try to keep your voice at a soft enough modulation that it's soothing, not grating. If the students all go to sleep, that can't be all bad.

On a pre-holiday day, you might say that the first person who bolts for the door or even asks whether he can go early will be given detention. Then do all you can with smiles and gentle assurances to keep those kids happy to be there. Or if it's desperate, let them out one minute early if every other teacher does. And be sure to wish them a pleasant holiday.

As a teacher or a sub, you have to get used to a certain amount of infantile behavior even in high school. In one classroom there were larger than lifesize cardboard likenesses of Wonder Woman and Superman tacked on the wall. Their arms and legs were fitted with brads so that their limbs could be adjusted. Almost inevitably, at each break between classes, each ended up clutching at his own genitalia, or were given a giant notebook paper bomber (a fake marijuana stogie) to hold. I came back after a break to find one boy stabbing Wonder Woman in the stomach with a spear. Unbelievable? I thought so. The spears and scimitars and others props, incidentally, were used for the speech classes. Another time, the beginnings of topic sentences for an essay which began: "For my first wish I would like _____; for my second wish I would like _____." All topic sentences for all three wishes were neatly filled in with "SEX". A little freshman girl was scandalized.

The teacher was in the hospital and a get-well card was being circulated for signatures, remarks and good wishes. Fellow teachers, students, administrators, campus aides, cafeteria staff — the whole range of the extended family wanted to express their concern for this very popular person. Colette wrote on the card, "Colette went skiing and broke three fingers." What an ego; did she think about anyone other than herself, ever? It was the most infantile approach I've ever seen to express regard for someone else's welfare.

"Charlie's molesting me." "How nice for you." "Charlie, this girl's complaining that you're not molesting her properly. I know you're only a freshman and have some time to learn in the next few years, but that's an area you're going to have to concentrate on." Everyone can laugh and it treats a situation with a deserved amount of importance. "Robert, you'll have to stop holding Jim's hand in class" or "Hey, you guys, unhand one another — save it for later" usually will stop the grab-ass (horseplay) before it gets out of hand. "He called me a fag!" "Remember, it takes one to know one." is another quick halt to a potentially explosive or disruptive situation.

"Knock it off!" when I was a boy meant STOP It must have gathered a sexual connotation also more recently. The phrase stops obstreperous freshman boys cold in their tracks. I just thought you'd like to know that.

If a student comes to you before class and tells you about some relatively minor transgreesion of the rules, he's anticipating getting busted for it; just listen patiently to him.

If a summons comes from the office during class time, take the time out then to advise him on how to deal with the situation. Have him slick his hair down, unrumple his clothing, stand at attention practically while he is in the presence of the VP, tell him to say, yes, sir, and no, sir, with assurances that he'll never do that terrible transgression again. And the kid will get off the hook, because the VP needs to know now and then that there are some changed souls out their in his bailiwick. The students in class need to know that someone is with them for reasonable advice when they need that, too. The kid and the rest of the class will learn the little lesson that surliness and rudeness will be rewarded differently from a more penitent manner. Something for everybody is my motto, and everybody gains.

When the sub is to administer testing, it's really helpful to have it all on a ditto. Blackboard use requires students to look up frequently and that complicates the proctoring problems. Incidentally, if the sub takes a position on the diagonal, there are fewer dead spots in the room. But never stay too stationary during an exam. Here again, a position at the back of the classroom for short periods can be calming.

For numbered exams, distribute the test booklets in order and collect them in order. No one may turn his in early or take it away for *any* reason. Otherwise, the exam is invalidated. Say, "Keep you test booklet and paper at your desk, your test paper face down. I will collect them at the end of the classhour." Allow about three minutes for this.

Watch the time carefully. Give students the exam as soon as you've taken roll and, of course, complete order is established. Give students the maximum time possible. If they tell you that they are always allowed to take exams in pairs, groups, or with open books, just say, "We'll be doing it differently this time."

To head cheating off at the pass, say "Each person must do his own. If there's cheating, the paper will be taken away." Say it matter-of-factly. Don't challenge someone else's class at this point. The first person who obviously defies the dictum on cheating; take his paper away and mark it: *cheating*; and assign detention. One of those does the trick usually. But repeat the dosage as necessary.

threatening atmosphere possible, so that students may do their best.

For a low-end group, you might say, "Okay, you guys, this is a test. You talk, I take." Some kids seem to like jingles and catch phrases, puns, plays on words. The more intelligent ones hate them and think them corny. Lower-range and younger students seem to really like catch phrases.

If a remark is made about someone as one who is heavily into drugs, ask the speaker which drugs, has he tried them, and how'd he like them? Divert the attention from the accusation (if the kid is an obvious goody-two-shoes) but if the accuser is the all-time loady — drop the whole thing and come on with pressure for getting on with the work at hand.

I came to the conclusion that the teachers who are absolutely inflexible about the roll — you're either in your seat when the bell rings or you're not; you're either in the class or not; etc. have the easiest time of it later. Despite the extra effort in the beginning, the word soon gets out that that is one of your hangups. It's easier to get a class going sooner for the sub, too; that's not one of the areas of discipline to challenge when the teacher is away.

In a way the teacher is saying, "be here, join us in this nice warm communion, don't stay away from us."

If a class gets really rowdy, say during the course of class; "This is the kind of thing that makes a substitute day really impossible. It's better if you go out of your way to promote a better atmosphere as this approach has accomplished nothing." Or, use the line I told you about before.

It's a pretty heavy guilt operation, but, in both instances, that kind of outrage was rewarded with instant calm. No one has ever even tried to tell them what it's like to be a substitute or has accused them of being bad hosts, apparently.

You have raised your voice to be heard, now return to your jellyfish. If anyone says something clever to cover the embarrassment of the situation, laugh and they will appreciate your forgiveness. Be sure to wish them all a pleasant day on leaving. You have made them reconsider and next time it will be better.

Only possible at the end of the classhour: "You know, we've really created a bad atmosphere here today. I'm sorry. Let's try it another way next time." Do they really want to go through another hour like this? No.

Kids often call or refer to the contentious teacher by his last name only. If you hear enough of this in reference to you, too, tone it down; you're coming on to strong(ly).

Be organized and ready to go like the person who has his keys ready when he gets into the car versus the one who fuddles endlessly before getting on the way.

Don't have a nip or smoke anything or take any other drugs to reduce the anxiety of being a substitute. It doesn't work. You're not as on-top-of-it as you need to be, and your classes won't go well. Instead, save it as a reward for having done as well as you could that day. You can't afford to seem dull-witted to students; they'll run all over you. At my wife's school, the VP had to carry a sub to his car. The sub was that drunk at 8 a.m.

Incidentally, there's a range of students who will contentedly and furtively roll let's pretend joints and casually leave them here and there to see what sort of reaction will follow a discovery. Obviously, the classmate who hurriedly pushes it into a pocket (intending to try it at home later), the more practiced types who roll it around between their fingers, and would smell it, smile, and drop it back, would be objects of great interest. A teacher, even a surrogate one, who freaks out over this sort of stuff is in for it. So that there is no mistaking this, the filling is usually pencil shavings or lawn cuttings, both of which if smoked, might be more harmful to your health than pot.

Don't let your phobias show:
If you're afraid of anything but flying or crowded freeways, don't let students know that. You'll think that St. Patrick himself has led all of his snakes to your classroom door if you tell students of your fear of them. The paper missiles will fly inevitably when the lights in your building go out and you have transmitted your fear of the dark vocally. You may have a rash of light failures, too. You have

just lost parent status and have become infantile in their eyes. They have gotten over that fear themselves and think that you should have too. You're just a case of retarded development, not a creative force to be dealt with. Go out of your way then to add a lilt to your voice and force yourself to smile even in the dark and that will be transmitted. Disguise your anxiety. Don't help create another generation of neurotics like you.

If it's only a dislike of something, like gum chewing, students can respect that; they'd better. You humiliate them publicly by making them spit it out in the wastebasket; you remark on it in class and assign detention; you discuss how declasse anyone is who has ever had such a thing in his mouth. Whatever your hangup or minor idiocyncracy, students will accept that. You're a little strange and old-fashioned anyway, but that too is a nice point of reference with their own older acquaintances, parents, and grand-parents.

The same hand gestures cannot be used by men and women. For instance, a man jerks his thumb toward the door to indicate to a student, "Out". (A woman must use a stiffened index finger and point toward the door instead.) For thumbs up (good, okay) she must use the thumb and forefinger O; for thumbs down (bad, failure) she turns her head to the side shaking it slightly, puts up a flattened palm which she also rocks gently from side to side. "T" for time-out for a man is his whole left and right hands stiffened to form the T; for a woman only the index fingers of each hand may be used. My wife field-tested these for me; and her kids complained when she did them my way. "This is not a game, Mrs. Brenot."

The detention supervisor told me that one teacher was not honoring my detention assignments and was effectively cancelling them through inaction. He said, "He's making a fool of you." which is a nice, ego-centered way of looking at it; but another possibility was that he had shot my control and power out from under me. I wouldn't sub for his classes again. Let somebody else get torn apart; it's just not worth it. The detention supervisor doesn't need to be the VP to avoid negative associations with it. It can be anyone on campus: an aide or a teacher. When a student questions his detention, as many will do; as the supervisor, don't get involved. Be neutral. You are neither the center nor the problem. That person needs to be honest and simply say, "I didn't make the assignments, how long are you here for? I'm doing it for the money; if you have any questions about it, go to the person who assigned it."

If you have a student designated to take the roll, who makes allowances for friends and fails to see and record their absences and tardies, announce that you will retake roll at the end of the classhour; and anyone missing then and not for an excused absence, will be assigned detention to make up the total time.

For a sub, low-expectation classes are very hard to control. There's a lot of dead-time in them, so you'd better be prepared with a song and dance act and/or a bullwhip. You must raise the expectations to conform to your own standard.

What should a sub wear? About one level more formal than the students and appropriate for your age, not theirs. However, don't wear a jacket and tie, or a designer suit, unless that is the standard of that district. School isn't a party, and everyone's more casual than before. If your attire is overkill, there's a range of student who will automatically want to "show" you. Wear modest clothing; wear underwear and bras. Watch the kids wearing punk rocker rigs; they're *always* behavior problems.

If some girl spends the bulk of the classhour putting on her makeup or reading a magazine, and you've told her several times to put whatever it is away, pick it up and dump it in the trash. She'll freak. If she says, "You can't do that.", Just say, "I just did it." She can get it out after class; and she'll stop doing that.

Relax and smile more. Students, like everyone else, like to be around people who are optimistic and happy. If you recognize a familiar face on campus, speak. Look into students' faces as you're walking along; and if you make eye contact, smile and nod slightly. They like to be remembered, too.

Some teenagers are very unrealistic. They don't understand that everyone doesn't make the $100,000 a year that their father, the plumbing contractor, does. They don't understand that one of these days they're going to have to make it on their own; some don't want to admit that one day they'll actually be middle-aged or old themselves. Most don't want to think about the fact that their parents are going to die one day. The first brush with death personally, and not in the abstract, often happens while a student is in high school. A classmate is mangled in a gory car crash or a grandparent dies. Many don't want to believe that life itself is a constant learning process. Don't be impatient with them; they'll get there eventually.

"I'd like to look like Bob Hope; he looks so young." (a student) I looked it up and Bob Hope was born on May 29, 1903. On his birthday in 1983, he was 80 years old. At 80, no matter what, you don't look young. Television and the movies have created an artificial reality for some of these kids.

Another aspect of the unreality of students is that they must think that any money you may earn (not get) as a result of being with them has either been like a gift (the contact has been that pleasant for you) or they have torn you apart and have shown you what can happen if for some reason they haven't liked you. Students often perceive their teachers quite oddly and unrealistically in other ways as well. They see them as capable of enjoying the solving of math problems at home in their spare time, willingly doing lab experiments in the garage on holidays and weekends, reading encyclopedias as frivolous and diverting entertainment. Some teachers have never been to a market, the bathroom, or any other usual and necessary spot on this earth.

Don't ever, even in the library, read a magazine or newspaper during class time (with the exception, naturally, of *Stop and Read*). They'll think that you're goofing off, ignoring them, and taking all of that money under false pretenses. They will automatically get noisier and restless. Instead, while you're in the library, help kids with the card catalogue, with finding resources on the shelves, circulate, and encourage them on. Stop the kids who are reading the sports page and sports magazines. (Why these choices rather than *House and Garden* readers as an example? They are generally the types who try to take advantage.) Why not let quiet dogs lie? The other kids hate to see their lazy brother get away with it. Even make an impromptu assignment for the one or two recalcitrant students who insist that they have all of the materials at home, and will finish the assignment that night. (Their mothers always have Ph.D.'s in the field and will help them.) There's also the one about the assignment being completed but forgotten at home and what a waste of time it would be to have to duplicate all of that effort. Or, how about, would you believe, "I left it in my other notebook."?

Teachers aren't being purposely malicious by sending those terrible lessons. They've either forgotten or have never subbed.

For an activities class: Take roll. Look at each student in the eye, have him raise his hand. You begin to make him personally responsible and an individual. Don't let students walk in, go to desks, benches, or tool boxes or have a student assistant take roll. You need to establish yourself. The regular teacher can do this only after he throughly knows his students and that takes more time than you have. You must be a new control entity and that can happen only when you demand it. Within five minutes most of those kids will be thoroughly engrossed in what they're doing, so the fact that there's a different control face will make no difference. But beware if you don't take the time for roll and some sort of introduction for the class. It can easily be a runaway. Some poor girl's face will get sprayed with *Pam* and some freshman's pants will be nailed to the workbench.

I heard an auto shop teacher tell a boy calmly and without any emotion at all that if the two bolts he was unscrewing came all the way out, the whole engine would crash down and crush the boy's body. That was nerves of steel, I'd call it. The sub is lucky to get bookwork.

With your opening monologue to a class, don't become a buffoon; try to model your delivery (not the material, the style) after Johnny Carson; a man with dignity, unbelievable timing, and a comfortable and reassuring sense of humor. Upper-range kids seem to like him, Chevy Chase and Gene Wilder types. With the lower ranges, you're on you own, but you can guess.

For student oral reports, move to the side of the classroom (front) with a tall stool, or stand there, or sit on a reversed writing desk. Stay elevated for control. Face diagonally so that you maintain total eye contact with the class and only peripherally with the speaker. For the regular teacher, he moves to the back of the classroom and forces the student making the presentation to become the instructor. The sub can't do that without losing control.

If students need to borrow a pen or pencil, always have them leave a hostage; otherwise you'll end up without a supply at all by the end of the day. Usually that cache has been built up slowly by the regular teacher's conservation and bendings over at the close of prior school days. It's unfair to squander someone else's effort by your indifference. When I was a boy we used the erasers on our pencils for corrections, not the dozens of bottles of liquid paper being used by everyone on campuses these days. There used to be a nice, old saying also, "Waste not, want not". It was right just enough of the time for me to keep believing it.

If paper balls start to fly at some sort of signal, or books drop or get slammed in unison, stop everything. Lean back against the desk or table and just look at the more aggressive ones. Say nothing but glance at your watch or the clock and wait. When all of this has subsided (and if you don't panic, it will end very shortly), just resume the lesson where you left off. That crisis is over, and you've just passed the test. Circulate with the trashbasket at the end of the hour; give the kids individual eye contact and a soft smile. You're okay.

To the library can mean goodbye to at least half the class, especially if it's some distance from the classroom. Some students think of the library as a very threatening and mysterious place, apparently; and one to be avoided. One kid told me that he had never been in one before, and he was a freshman in high school. I asked him after the orientation what he thought about it, and he wrinkled his nose. The library assistant's pacing was too fast and simply compounded the confusion.

When you take a class to the library, unless you're in a very contained building, announce before leaving that each student is to check out with you at the end of the hour. Take the roll sheet with you and rather than marking directly on it, overlay a blank lined sheet, line it up and tick the kids off. If there's slippage, do your own detention slips. Always double the time. The more of this sort of thing you do early on, the easier it will be on successive days.

For student accountability in an activity class, this technique has been effective: (To the student) You will receive points for attendance each day (or today for a sub) as follows:

4 points if you do the class activity all period
3 points if you do that for half the period
2 points if you did an assignment or homework for another class
1 point if you were in class
Misbehavior can be penalized with negative points.
These points will be added at the end of the grading period and will be a part of your overall grade alone with your various project grades.

Brenot's Unembellished Observations of Who's Paying the Bill:

1. *Children misuse their clothing right up to the very day when they have to buy their own.*
2. *Students tend to take better care of the lab equipment, texts, and tools that they have either paid a deposit on or own themselves.*
3. *The children of the richest parents in the community don't waste anything. The kid who can least afford it wastes the most. The waste extends to time as well as things.*
4. *Teenage sons' appetites only wane after they have moved away from home and have to pay for their own food.*

Beware of the Ides of March and April and of the Lunchroom. If you thought the Hindu caste system of old was inflexible, try sitting at "the coachs' table". When they find that your area of expertise is not every game score and player profile from the American, National, and peanut leagues, your conversational career with them will come to an abrupt halt. You may as well move away from them, your untouchable status is irreversible.

The English and foreign language departments usually hole up in their offices and develop a cliqueishness that's almost impenetrable for an outsider. Too often the foreign language people maintain their exclusivity by speaking only the non-English tongue to one or two others. The music people (except for a band master now and then) are loners and will leave when the faculty comes en masse.

You then have the option of the "women's table", "the fun and games" types, the office workers, a random custodian or campus aide, and maybe another lonely substitute. It's too often just another miserable time.

Stop to think about it, perhaps you're better off bringing a book or magazine and staying in your last classroom by yourself (at least you can't be insulted or ignored there), or leaving campus and parking under a tree somewhere away from it all.

Some subs produce their credentials like fold-out wallet pictures and try to promote themselves with a hard sell. It puts people off. Cool it instead. Remember, teachers having lunch are not employment recruiters. They're not going to recommend you for a job or anything else after this sort of meeting. Their interest in your past career is indifference at best.

The "room environment" of the teachers' rooms I've seen could be the subject of an interesting study. Collectively, their style runs to Late-Black-Hole-of-Calcutta. They are usually dank, gloomy interior, institutional, close to garbage cans, and filled with castoffs or molded plastic. They're not exactly designed to create a nice mood or the lightening of the spirit. They're too often just depressing and quite inhospitable.

The Seating Chart for Lunch: Please be seated, table hopping, and lapping it up at lunchtime.

Pity the poor sub who isn't aware of the groupings and sub-species which form at lunchtime and who blunders into the wrong pew. For your information, there are:

The Macho Table
> Coaches (of everything except dance and drama)
> Math teachers
> Science teachers
> Industrial Arts teachers

Even though the table size will not expand, the circle will grow as large as necessary to accommodate them all. Everyone will be pushed-over-for who's a member of the gang. Their discussions will revolve around topics of sports, primarily teams (but their own personal and family sports activities, as well), and SCHOOL. Many of these people have alternative careers so that school is only one part of their day. They tend to make it a point of knowing a lot of people around town. They tend to have some well-placed jibes and barbs aimed strategically at the administrative jugular, which rise to a crescendo around contract renegotiation time. The most extremely contentious types will sit here with the others.

The Rowdies, Widows, and Orphans Tables
> Social Studies teachers
> Special interest: Librarian, Speech Therapist, the Nurse
> Home Economics teachers
> Womens' P.E. teachers (unless a math or science major)
> Fine or Performing Arts (sometimes)

Groupings vary widely in this buffer zone. Most of the people hare are: displaced housewives (who often see school as a living, not as an end in itself. As the French say, "I work to live, not live to work."), one-of-a-kinders, newly arrived and insecure (first year teachers and subs), and those who have enough complications in their lives and need some diversion. They will discuss anything other than school; e.g., their families, what's happening worldwide, nationally, on TV, raunch; they rely on an off-handed, free flow. Table groupings vary considerably but tend to enlarge from fours when they push tables together to accommodate new members. This is the most heterogeneous and amorphous grouping of the three. There are few fixed positions.

The Academicians
> Foreign language teachers (when lured from their lairs)
> English teachers (ditto — although many use every lunch hour to try to catch up on their overload of papers)
> Social Studies teachers (more serious types)
> Fine and Performing Arts (sometimes)
> Academic Old-Timers (often those who have been in the district longest stay in their rooms by themselves.

These people see school as their careers, generally. They tend to have little patience with those who are not devoted professionals, those who are too genuinely critical (the Academicians complaints are usually quite superficial and trivial, actually), or those they perceive of as not taking it all seriously enough. They spend a great deal of their time discussing individual students, or "the finer things of life", or the play they have just seen. They do not welcome the less cultivated. Seating is limited; if you miss the first sitting, you are out of luck. Regulars will tolerate only one stranger already seated before they shift their base of operations to another area of the room. The others will follow.

For the sub it would be helpful to have the areas roped off and clearly labeled with the RESERVED markers in place.

To the Teacher:

How about considering conducting a conversation with a substitute on any topic other than who he's trying to pretend to be today? He must have some other sort of identity that might be interesting to hear something about, too. It might be worth a try.

It's not all serious stuff at school. I found myself writing the reason for David's truancy and detention was that: "he was 48 minutes late" for a fifty minute class.

If you goof something up pretty badly and get caught out, you can always fall back on that old dodge, "I was just testing to see whether you were paying attention." Say it with a broad smile. Most kids will like that one.

You can't help not to appreciate remarks like, "Ah, Mr. Brenot, returning to the scene of the crime, I see." from an ex-compatriot.

I had gotten poison oak on my chin and was slathered with salve, so the teacher leaned over the lunch table and said, sotto voce, "Aren't you glad they've found a cure for herpes?"; to which I answered, "I wondered why you seemed so happy today."

One school has an "Opportunities" Class for kids kicked out of regular classes. Opportunity for what? "To improve their behavior," I was told, "or they are out on the street."

107

From a school handbook under the heading: Discipline, Supervision, and Health, "Be sure that proper respect is given to the lunch tables and benches." At ease, private.

I had accepted the job of substituting for that day very early as the district was highly organized and called ahead of time as much as possible. Only when I went out to the car much later did I discover that our seventeen year old cat had climbed into the back of my car and was in the process of dying. I called the district answering service to tell them that I wasn't going to be able to come after all, as I simply couldn't disturb our dying cat. It didn't seem at all strange to me at the time, only later when I mentioned the incident to someone who remarked that, "I'll bet they thought that was a new one in excuses."

The very shy pre-adolescent boy was reading aloud in class the father's part from the play version of *The Diary of Anne Frank*. Unfortunately, his eye skipped down one line to the next speaker's part and he read instead of cat, "You've been in your room playing with your (Pieter)." That brought the house down.

"Is the gas in your stomach inflammable?" (a student) "Is my writing edible?" (another student) "Those things hanging down from a cow; is one for milk, and one for cream, and one for cheese, or just how does that work?" (still another student) "How's Mark doing?" (a parent) "He's trying in both senses of the word." (a teacher)

Schools have nice people who are fun to be with. Maybe that's another reason why I felt compelled to write this. If more people could feel free to relax and enjoy a nicer atmosphere, they might be happier to be with one another, also.

To recap: What can a sub do?

1. Request administrative approval to assign detention yourself.

2. In your advice to the teacher on how the day went: (a) Give an honest accounting of the day; (b) Advise the teacher how to improve the lesson for sub days.

3. Be patient with regular teachers; they really don't know what they're doing to you by their attitudes, style with classes, and the character of their lessons. Don't put up with their not honoring your detention assignments, however. That's not playing it straight.

4. Review what was said or done that triggered any volatile behavior or a really nice response. Eliminate antiquated slang or anything that may have gotten a bad laugh. Review your own vocal quality for irritating tone or mannerisms.

5. Think back about what went right and wrong and think of ways to improve a flawed situation in case that or something similar comes up again, and have a really nice day.

The Parent Conference, Homework, and God Bless Our Happy Home

Let's play: Pin the Parents on Their Progeny, or is that the other way around? Translation: What's going on here? "For years now, the problem with schools has been kids." (an ex-teacher jokingly) "What my generation thought of as basic: food, clothing, shelter, and education has now added as basic: sex, and drugs, and rock and roll" (a parent). "I'm glad you called and told me about my daughter's snotty behavior." (a parent) A teacher told me that she had sent a note home which said, "Please help Victor with his spelling; he's fallen behind." The reply came back the next day, "If Victor doesn't work hard, beat him." "I did marvelous on the English Proficiency Exam." (a parent) After the hearing and sight exams had been given schoolwide, the health aide called the father to report that his son's test results indicated weakness and that she recommended further testing. The father asked, "Is that the reason he doesn't do well in P.E.?" Was he concerned about the limitations on the boy's academic prowess? "How would you have liked to have a child like Leonardo da Vinci in class? Can you imagine an Italian schoolroom with even one child as gifted as that?" (a teacher) "Billy Williams is the boy who is in detention daily and

109

seems proud of it. He never walks, he swaggers. After spitting on one boy, he wadded up his detention notice; and threw it in the teacher's face. He's pre-prison, you know." (a teacher) "Today was my birthday; I got to stay home from school." (a student)

Early in the game it was the parents who bought the candy, cookies, cupcakes, crackerjack, and cokes as treats for their children. They conditioned their kids also too often to having unrealistic expectations of what "everybody" else had, was doing, was getting. And then the complaints. My kids are lazy, shiftless, self-centered, non-directed. They don't know the value of money, how hard I've had to work for everything we have, or do they appreciate . . . etc. No kidding. "The more I buy the happier I get." (a student) "I want it all and I want it now." (a bumper sticker) "Think Greed." (another bumper sticker)

If they could do it over again, how many parents would do it quite differently? Some of them still haven't learned, however. How many parents of teenagers know what their children are really doing and thinking anyway?

As far as I can think back, every teenager's lifestyle has been unacceptable to his parents' generation. Have you noticed that the parents inevitably feel that the current standard is always so much lower than in their youth? I remember when Frank Sinatra was considered declasse, sleazy, and quite unacceptable to my family. My family tended to be supporters of the Bing Crosby sound instead. Old Wave always was preferred over the new. And Sinatra had greasy hair in those days; tut, tut. (We were an interesting group of hopeless snobs.) Jitterbugging was immoral; and Sloppy Joe sweaters (a cardigan worn backwards so that your boobs protruded more obviously) and anklets were unspeakably undecorous for nice, young ladies, too. That was often enough a subject at the dinner table — our high standards.

Let's Play: Pin the Tale on the Principle: Cheaters never prosper.

Cheating is another standard that I've had to review. I would have told you not too long ago that I was opposed to it in every way. It robbed the person who did it of satisfaction in doing something for himself; it indicated low self-esteem, a lack of accomplishment; and it robbed him of dignity. Now I'm not so sure. There are just too many examples of people who cheat and not only get away with it, but prosper. How many teachers have felt that the grade line was a little skimpy and have added several average grades of the assignments he had corrected, to fill in the spaces here and there? I've told several little white lies in my day (but only for someone else's good, mind you). Who hasn't constructed a totally phony bibliography or two. There was always that rumor that some old prof had caught someone out; I wonder who circulated that one year after year to the incoming freshmen? Doctors pull plugs reportedly; women wear girdles and falsies. I've read that policemen, despite their oath, rarely stop to ticket a speeding car which has a mix of scruffy-looking Black and Anglo passengers. In percentages, they get blasted too frequently; and they're not eager to create some more widows and orphans; their own.

If you know it's not right, don't do it; but if it is, go for it with gusto. It's as simple as the family that lays together, stays together; or the family that smokes together, croaks together. One thing seems to lead to another.

It's the early bird that gets the worm; it's the early worm that gets eaten, too.

And time passed as it tends to do. And times past as they never were often are fondly remembered (another unexpected divertisement, a Haydn Surprise). I'm just having some fun.

Now, back to those "high standards" — I have since wondered if they were so high that a lot of people in the world were totally unaware they even existed. In others words, we were talking to ourselves, alone, and maybe for good reason. If you're all that superior yourself, how do you ever find enough worthies as friends? Exclusivity often breeds isolation and loneliness.

The "noise" from a swing band playing on the radio was enough to send my grandfather out of a room with his hands clasped over his ears. That was a violent reaction for him. Since then, there have been such dubious tastemakers as Elvis the Pelvis in the 50's, Jimmy Hendrix and Janis Joplin with their heavy drugs in the 60's, Johnny Rotten and the Sex Pistols, Alice Cooper killing chickens on stage in the 70's; and then there are those new groups for the 80's. How many parents are able to say honestly, "What an interesting new sound." How much of a teenager's interest in the "unacceptable" is heightened simply because few parents, with their exalted standards rooted firmly in yesteryear, could say that? But they have forgotten and quite handily, too, the impact of their own misguided youth on their parents. If your beer busts are today's pot parties, what is tomorrow going to bring you might ask? And notice how legitimate some of those former scourges of society have generally become.

See Spot run? Not any more, he won't — poor old fellow. He's hopelessly crippled now and half-blind. Run over by a semi. I had a nice, warm place in my heart for Spot. He was one of the first words I learned to read; and I was so excited. Why is so much that happens during the teen years designed to revolt the older generation? We did (or tried to) do the same, as I recall.

Why did properly trained Victorians leave a dab of each dish on the plate? (Answer: To show that they had had enough dinner.) When I was a kid we were told that you only said, "Would you like *some*?" (never *more* or *enough* either.) One was not to call attention to the quantity that someone else might consume. Wow! Social pitfalls galore. We can't assume that all of these little lessons that our parents gave us so freely, ought not be reviewed for their relevancy today. Leaving dabs of food was a terrible waste, and the practice generally died out during the rationing of World War II.

How much of the lesson is either relevant or desirable? When the home economics teacher spends time instructing the class on table etiquette and on how to set a table properly, how properly is properly? Is she simply perpetuating some unnecessary and useless standard passed on to her? Why is a napkin supposed to have the fold toward your body? Why do you serve cream soups in a cup and use a round bowl spoon, a broth in a wide and flat bowl and use a dessert spoon? Why is your left hand supposed to be in your lap when you're not cutting something? Why do forks have tines if you're not allowed to stab, but must shovel from the side, instead? Why does the dessert fork have to go in a particular direction? These are not earth-shattering issues, but many parents and teachers have made them the equivalent. We don't need troughs for all; but we might review and revise and adopt a standard that may make better sense for today. I've even got a slogan: Eschew those mountains of trifles! The same might be said for some other areas of the curriculum also. But whatever became of the four basic food groups of my youth? Now that may be one standard from yesteryear worth returning to.

If a lot of adolescent anit-social behavior (drugs, pornography, excessive booze, etc.) is the result of a lack of physical touching at a very young age by an egocentric, fearful, tentative and unstable parent; then if people become even more narcissistic, cold, and self-centered, concerned with themselves and the things they've surrounded themselves with, wouldn't future generations be in for even higher crime rates if those no-no's stay illegal? To try to reverse this, maybe we ought to consider as one aspect of a new educational approach, schools for parents. Every parent relies so strongly on what he learned as a child, adds a few other experiences to that, and essentially plays child-raising by ear. Has any parent ever been told that it's essential for him to touch his children frequently to avoid later anti-social behaviors?

Equal time is unnecessary, but some time is. Perhaps we ought to balance a *Violence In America* video program with what should parents do if their children misbehave and make them angry. What are the best things that parents can do in a given situation to re-program unacceptable approaches: theirs and their children's? Invest some energy and make it entertaining. Everyone needs to fulfill certain tests and prove the competency of some skills just to get a driver's license, but there are no qualifications whatever for becoming a parent. Almost everyone can do it. Driver's qualifications are said to have saved lives as it has kept the inept off our roads, but we haven't devised a way as yet to keep the inept out of our nation's beds, however.

Gor some kids, holidays are not exactly pleasant times

always. They're locked away with their parents for a week or two; their mobility is often sharply curtailed. There's no excuse for being gone for twelve to fourteen hours at a stretch and there are always those questions about things they really don't want to be questioned about, think, or talk about. There must be a couple of things from your past that you're not too proud of and would rather have forgotten too. A holiday can be traumatic. If they have drunken, neglectful, or brutalizing parents, so much the worse. School, the haven, looks pretty good to some of these students. Their bad feelings must be even more bitter as they see classmates with sugarplums. Would you look forward to St. Valentine's Day with relish if there were a guaranteed mob-style massacre each year?

What student could help but be confused by parental inconsistency? What parent hasn't wanted his child excused from school while the family has visited Barbados? It's an exception to the rigid requirement that his children must be in school each day. They may leave by Pan-Am, be waved through customs, be met by a hotel or company rep with limousine, be whisked to a secluded resort (with a staff of thousands) far away from any native influence, where they eat American food, drink bottled water out of fear of the local amoeba, etc. That's a kind of foreign culture; and that's more broadening than staying at home, they keep saying. Anyway, they want their kids to be excused from school for that.

Now It's Time For Our Nutrition Break:

If you know it's not true, don't keep saying it.
If you don't like it, don't buy it.
If you know it's not good for you, don't eat it.

When I was a boy, we learned about the four basic food groups and were expected to choose something from each category every day. Food as I recall had a purpose. It was to nourish your body and make you grow.

Excerpt from a student, "I like many different types of food. Like any other kid, I like candy. I like chocolate

114

candy like Hershey's, Mr. Goodbar, and Watchamacallits, and Krackels. I like Bubble-Yum, Juicy Fruits bite-size, and more. I like bite-size candy like M&M's, Jolly Ranchers, Reese's Pieces, Skittles, Jujyfruits, Junior Mints, and more . . . I love chocolate eclairs. I like them with vanilla custard in them. I like Suzy-Q's, donuts, and I love ice cream. I love pies, chocolate cream pie, and banana cream pie; I crave apple pie, peach . . ."

If you know it's not right, don't keep doing it. The sugar on the top of cafeteria breakfast coffee cake, washed down by hot chocolate, is enough to make the calmest student wired and hyper for at least the first couple of classes. How come school dieticians haven't caught on to what their compatriots in other areas seem to be saying, "Less sugar, calmer people"? And what about some of those other government surplus foods: Bologna, corn dogs, turkey roll, margarine? Is this a conspiracy to poison the next generation systematically? At one school there is a boy who carries a pocket full of sugar cubes to "tide himself over" during the school day. Of course, he's bouncing off the walls most of the time; and, of course, his parents are "concerned" about his behavior. How about that?

When, in one district, the Board outlawed empty un-foods like blip and blip (those unnamed, ersatz-cream filled pasteries), those appeared daily for months after the deadline for buying *new* ones. The school had a *lot* of old ones on hand, yummy and appetizing, cracked icing and all. Now, was that an example of a) poor administrative planning, b) a quantity discount, c) a finger or two in the cookie jar, or d) a whole hand or two in the cookie jar? How much do you think that bribe will cost us taxpayers? If the dietician was more concerned with the bottom line, the cafeteria profit, than with the health of the children of that district, what was that person being paid to do? Some of these people defy credibility.

I've saved an article with a quotation from the ITT subsidiary, Continental Bakery President G. Michael Hostage. (L.A. Times, Tuesday, December 9, 1980, in an article by Bill Sing, Times Staff Writer) . . . "Controversy over Twinkies' nutritional value, he says, comes from 'nothing more than misunderstanding the role of different food products in the diet.'"

115

"No one ever claimed, for example, that one should be prepared to live on a diet of potato chips and soft drinks and expect to be healthy. Hostess Twinkies and cup cakes are snack foods. We'd be the last to claim, I think, that anyone should eat these food products in order to get any specific diet or health value."

"But, on the other hand, they're not bad to eat. They're fun to eat, and we sell them as fun foods. They're eaten because they're simply pleasurable."

What is the definition of food and maybe that's what's going wrong for my understanding. What I'm hearing, and correct me if I'm wrong, is that Mr. Hostage is saying, too, that ITT never claimed that Twinkies had nutritional value; they're fun food.

My understanding was that to be called food, whatever it was, had to nourish, to make grow, and if ITT's products don't do that, perhaps they need to be called something else other than food. It seems to me that fun has become somewhat perverted in certain circles if they are willing to squander our youth and burn out their bodies on empty calories for their profit. Their unconfirmed target for 1980's Twinkie production was one billion, which the author of another article pointed out if stretched end to end would circle the globe twice at the equator with enough left over to stretch from Los Angeles to New York. That's a lot of fun and profit.

In Alan Sampson's book, *The Sovereign State of ITT*, he pointed out that ITT maintained production facilities in Hitler's Germany and made products there that were used against the Allies during World War II. What a strange coincidence. It was hard for ITT to lose no matter who won or lost that war. As my algebra teacher would have put it, they took a firm stand on the fence.

Now if ITT's historical patterning is consistent, we'd do well to watch closely any investment move they make into nation's X, Y, or Z. They may know something we don't as yet.

"Blimey," said the duchess. If only the Duchess of Windsor had said that instead of her frequently reported remark, "A woman can be neither too rich nor too thin". In all, the most patently stupid remark to come from a person who ought to have been a little more aware of the gullibility of the public out there in fantasyland. I wonder what her IQ was? Did anyone ever stop to consider that she was only half right anyway, and a really rich widow *is* irresistible, but Buchenwald-style bodies are too thin? Anorexia is not pretty. Is it attractive to starve to death?

Did the Duchess ever say that a woman could be neither too rich nor too young? And, by definition, one can be too young to be a woman. But how old was she when she made that preposterous and childish remark? But why did so many people fall for that sort of ridiculous bullshit anyway? Why, also, are Americans so hung up on being discontented with their ages? Why is younger better, supposedly, when those of us who are not there, but are older (I'm 50) know better than that? Maturity is another dimension in life. Survival and being here, contributing something, and enjoying yourself is, I'm sure, better than being dead and not here and not having some nice, and interesting, and new experiences.

Anorexia is not an upper-class disease at all. It cuts through all class lines but you would expect truly upper-class women to be a little more self-assured than the Duchess was apparently; remember, she was not to the manor born. She married well was the way they used to put it when I was a boy.

Rather, anorexia seems to be a phenomenon for those who want to ape their betters, or at least those they think have more money – or are thinner – than they.

Adolph Hitler caused a bit of a stir in the civilized world just a few years ago, as I recall, because of his involuntary anorexic policy. People didn't seem too thrilled with Buchenwald bodies in those days. Hitler's victims didn't exactly go willingly to their deaths, either. The conditions were actually quite different, only the results weren't.

I've heard of Napoleons, Beef Wellington, Lady Baltimore Cake, Oysters Rockefeller, Peach Melba, a Sandwich of any kind – but I don't think that either the Duchess or Hitler is going to be remembered for any special flavor treat. Duchesse potatoes were not named in her honor. The Culinary Hall of Fame (or Shame, depending on your tastes) will have passed them by.

At least the Duchess had good taste, a lot better than

that gradiose kitsch that Hitler specialized in and built all over Germany. His projects were very upscale and terribly Louis the 17th. Can you imagine that the West German government actually spent money to restore some of those buildings following the war's bomb damage? I wonder what fund that came out of and who really paid the bill?

Remember it was Adolph Hitler who demolished the Bauhaus School, the very group dedicated to simplifying our lives, and in creating with the machine aesthetically pleasing things to live with. Imagine some of the interesting objects and lifestyles that might have been suggested by the Bauhaus brains using the machine's brawn. Hitler thought that that taste range was decadent but have you ever seen photos of the junk he liked? He had nerve, a monumental conceit, trying to pass himself off as either a dictator, or a lover, or an artist, or a tastemaker. He didn't do anything well from what I've read. "Was Hitler a good guy or a bad guy?" (a student)

I wonder when the final tally is in historically, though, which one will have done more damage than the other. Hitler is credited with approximately 30 million dead. I haven't been able to get figures on the current numbers of anorexics, or on the numbers of people who have fallen for the latest fad diets, or are existing primarily on fun foods, and, of course, future health problems can only be surmised.

Can you imagine how much work it must have taken the Duchess to be included on the annual "best-dressed" list year after year? What incredible narcissism! That's a lot of time spent on how you look. And then to let your body disintegrate under the pretty wrapping seems ludicrous. It's insane. Can you imagine the Duchess in a mini-bikini?

The Duchess made that fatuous remark only when she was quite old herself and beyond the age when a two-piece bathing suit of any kind would have been appropriate anyway.

If the Duke got an annual stipend from the British government and the Duchess squandered it on a lot of clothing which became almost instantly outdated, weren't they welfare cheats on a grand scale but of the lowest sort? If I had been a taxpaying member of British society, I would really have resented that kind of subsidy to someone who wasted my efforts so flagrantly. She could pay for her clothing out of all the money she saved from buying food. Her priorities were a bit confused from my point of view.

Old peoples' skin loses a layer of fat and they tend to wear more clothing to compensate and stay warm. They frequently overheat their hourse, a time in their lives when they're usually on a fixed income and they can least afford the added expense. That enclosed setting all too often becomes a cage of loneliness and isolation and as their protective defenses are weakened, they become more prone to other diseases as well. It's another vicious circle and one that seems especially strange that younger people would adopt voluntarily even a part of. And why waste purposely our limited natural resources?

As a humanities type, your mind runs off on strange little tangents sometimes. But often enough to keep you encouraged, there is the possibility of some truth in your meanderings and so you forge ahead.

You must have layers of fat on your body to store fat soluble vitamins (like A, D from the sun, E and K; and E is the healing vitamin). Layers of fat are also necessary for holding your internal organs in place and keep you from feeling cold. It's nature's own way of regulating your well-being. No pill is able to do all of that so far. Obesity isn't reasonable, either; it puts too much strain on your heart. Over 600,000 people die each year in the U. S. from heart attacks; and only one-third of them are men. But there's a stage that is a little fuller and more rounded than the current style in vogue that makes people look better to me. Women who look drawn and vacant somehow, no matter how much make-up tries to disguise it, don't look rich to me. They just look foolish instead for falling for such an idiotic and bizarre notion as that of the Duchess.

Here's a riddle: If a lot of anorexics have been created because they abhor real food, how long would someone last who ate nothing but "fun food"?

Postulates 1 and 2 and 3:

By the time food has a shelf-life of one year, it has only the appearance of being fresh.

At least a TV dinner has the appearance of being a balanced meal.

If the bread will not mold, how can it support life? That's an interesting experiment for the whole family to do.

Anyway, the Duchess and her insecurities have done a lot of damage. Even some teenage boys have gotten on the Buchenwald bandwagon.

Right now at least ten percent of all women over fifty have osteoporosis (a disintegration of the bones which then become brittle and don't heal if injured) which is caused by a lack of calcium. Figures range anywhere from 10% to 50% depending on the source. These women grew up at a time when diets were better than now; they could be victims of the poverty of the Depression; a lot of possibilities actually.

Unless you're really into pain, can you imagine the agony of having bones in your body that have disintegrated? (I wonder if that kind of disintegration is similar to the bones left in a can of salmon, mackerel, or sardines? The first leper I ever say was in Nepal, and he was scary.) All too typically the expensive medicines don't really do very much. And how would you mask the torture of damaged bones with a pain killer anyway? Can medicines like that kill pain selectively and locally, or are they killing you or your pain over all your body?

In a survey of student diets, out of two classes totalling seventy-six students in a two day period: seven had milk once at dinner, 17 had milk two days at dinner, only 24 at all had milk and that's slightly less than one-third of the total. And that was the major meal of the day, not a more typical fun food pick-up lunch. Incidentally, less than 30% of the total had any salad or vegetables in that same two day period.

"The reason I don't drink milk is that it's fattening and I want to stay thin." (a student) But milk isn't the only source of calcium by any means, but where is the calcium in too many of the Killer menus which follow? (All dairy products including yogurt, almonds, and sardines are good sources of calcium.)

How long can you last on fun food? Some of the menus from those students will come pretty close to zero-basing real food, too. Lunch is too typically just so much

120

fun food; a lot of people skip breakfast or have a sweet liquid diet drink; so where is all of the real food going? Is that a genuine commie plot? I wonder if the Soviets made fun food out of all of that grain we sold them? They eat real food and stay strong and healthy and mentally alert, while we get fun food. And our weapons-systems keep getting more technically sophisticated while the people who run them become less and less mentally capable. It doesn't make sense. "What do electric trains run on; it can't be steam, can it?" (a student) "What would happen if I stepped out of an airplane? Could I sit on a cloud?" (another student) In an analysis on the draftees of the 60's, it was said that even then only one-third of our male youth were mentally, emotionally, or physically eligible for the draft. Imagine what that figure is now.

"I wished I could be a model, be tall but not too tall, also be very thin; then I could be very rich." (a student) We must have raised a generation of nutritional illiterates and that's fatal not just difficult. I don't think the four basic food groups of my youth have been changed, or people's capacity to absorb nutrients has changed. And it hasn't changed that you must have a balance in your diet to make you grow and stay healthy. What may have changed is that there are no nutrients to absorb in too many of the foods mentioned. Now, how much sugar, sodium, and saturated fat; the Big Three Killers without anything to balance them off; do these kids' diets have anyway?

Consider what must be happening to the body formation of the children whose dinners are like these night after night. These are sample menus from 8th graders. This is an age when more families, than later on very often, have a sit-down meal together as a family; later it's too typically every-man-for-himself on-the-run. These menus are complete; there are no foods taken for granted like milk, rolls and butter, salad, vegetables. Read them, they're astounding and frightening. This is dinner, the main meal for most of them:

steak, potatoes, water;
french toast with syrup, sausage, milk, and chocolate cookies;
did not have dinner;
pizza and a coke;

pizza with pepperoni and a coke;
turkey, milk, and ice cream;
burrito and a coke;
yogurt, chips, and a coke;
hot dogs, milk, chips;
hot dog, chips and fruit punch;
hamburger, french fries, and chocolate milk;
hamburger, fries, frosty;
macaroni and cheese and orange juice;
a taco, onion rings, and orange juice;
an egg sandwich;
a sandwich, cake, milk;
a fried egg sandwich, pudding (with ersatz cream topping) and milk;
a baked potato;
nothing;
breaded fish sticks, peas, apple juice;
two children listed chewing gum as a food and six listed Twinkies.

These children are not from poor families; they are solid middle-class. It doesn't seem to be a question of how much food costs, because a lot of the foods mentioned were packaged or prepared.

Who said that junior high age students ought to eat a disproportionately high percentage of carbohydrates for calming down?

If I were a junior high teacher, I would insist on a new paint job if necessary, and I would wear nothing but a male version of bubble-gum pink if that is the most relaxing color around and require all kids that age to wear that same colored uniform to school.

I don't want to bore you with much more, but those diets are not an adequate quantity for their age, balanced, or even good tasting. If this breadbasket-of-the-world nation of ours can't get its nutritional act together, then future generations are going to be seriously affected. Imagine the expensive diseases these kids are going to have in their old age. Osteoporosis move over; company's coming! If I were a betting man, my stock market tip to everyone would be to buy heavily in old-folks, "convalescent" hospitals and pharmaceuticals. You might not have to wait very long to get a healthy return on that investment.

If this generation gets wiped out financially because of ill-health later on, how long will it take then for pressure to build in demanding an expensive national health system?

Real food and artificial vitamins are not the equivalent, either. Despite the Monsanto Company's attempt to democratize all chemicals, they are not always equal. Some vitamins must be taken in combination with one another in order to be absorbed by the body. That process occurs naturally in foods; it doesn't always when the vitamins are introduced synthetically. A pill may not do it for us after all.

If the Tea and Toast Syndrome demolishes brain cells of oldsters, who then become senile in two to three months on the tea and toast variety of diet, aren't some of these children's food combinations almost the equivalent; Is it any wonder that these kids are not doing as well academically in school today as students of only a decade ago? What teachers don't complain frequently of that little reality? National test scores declining each year? Student performance peaked for me personally in the late 60's when a lot of people were hung up on their diets and natural foods. It's been downhill ever since. Students today may not have the capacity genuinely to do any better. They may have zero-based their brain power with the terrible range of fun foods available at your fiendly local supermarket. That was not a printing error, either.

Do you remember that great recipe quoted in *Eating May Be Hazardous To Your Health*?

> water, sugar, nonfat dry milk and whey solids with calcium hydroxide and disodium phosphate, modified tapioca starch, hydrogenated vegetable oil, cocoa processed with alkali, emulsifiers (sodium stearoyl-2-lactylate, polysorbate 60, and sorbitan monostearate), artificial color and flavor, sodium caseinate, salt, dextrose, carrageenan, guar gum

Hands up for fun foods. All of those things are ingredients in packaged chocolate pudding. If you can't pronounce it, don't eat it.

The *Fortune* magazine for January 24, 1983 tells us in an article about "The New Technology of the Mind" that thirty-five million Americans (about 16%) suffer from mental disorders ranging anywhere from sleeplessness to senile dementia. Now, what do you think may have caused or contributed significantly to those problems? *Fortune* suggests increased revenues and even more enormous profits for the drug companies in the future. I have a more modest proposal and encourage everyone to get his drugs at his friendly local supermarket instead in the form of a well-balanced selection of fresh foods. Then we may see some real change in behavioral patterns and mental capacities. Do you recall hearing people talk about brain foods when you were a child, foods like fish and other seafoods? Perhaps when the Catholic Church dropped the weekly requirement for seafood (or at least non-meat) for Fridays, that was not a favor to parishioners at all.

Both my wife's and my grandmothers always said, when we asked for something to eat before dinner, "If you're really hungry, have a piece of bread and butter." In those days, bread was real whole wheat and the butter not some synthetic spread, also. I didn't mention food quality in conjunction with the students' dinner menus, but that's another whole topic. Bread and butter had a calming effect. You weren't supposed to fill up on sweets or fun foods before you had the important nutrients. Dessert was last and a reward for finishing everything else. But what if the meal is primarily dessert, salty, or oily, as many of those students' meals were?

Incidentally, what are schools doing in the area of nutrition? Typically, nothing. Courses in survival? Can you imagine a curriculum which would ignore sex education, nutrition, consumer education, and exercise?

I understand that some of the military services are now contracting food services out to civilian companies rather than maintaining control in-house. I hope that subsidiaries of ITT and Monsanto aren't among the contractors or suppliers of "foods". If our military zero-bases food and fun food or the equivalents become the norm, then we're really in trouble. Maybe some KP is worth it after all.

If we know that nutrition changes behavior; if we know that nutrition affects our capacity to learn; if we know that sound nutritional practices are essential for our very survival, then why are we playing little games instead of taking it all a little more seriously? If you know it's wrong, don't do it.

If you don't know anything about nutrition, the

Safeway supermarket chain has several from a series of excellent *and* free brochures that can guide you. It wouldn't do any harm to anyone to read them selectively.

"Children are so carefree; they have no real worries." (an adult) "My teenage years were the happiest of my life." (another adult)

The Student Body, Activities, and God Bless Our Happy Home

Here we go again, our happy home. It conjures up a nice Norman Rockwell sort of feeling, doesn't it? The reality is a little different, unfortunately. Tom Lehrer came pretty close to the mark when he sang, "Be it ever so decadent, there's no place like home." But let's have these sweet children say it in their own words, their own inimitable style, I believe the saying goes. These are mostly 8th graders, also; by high school, students have become more circumspect and secretive and usually avoid writing anything they feel may at any time be used against them. As they get older, they also get less volatile emotionally: less hate and more dislike, less ecstatic and more very happy; they calm down. These kids are pretty out front so be forewarned.

To be an effective teenager has become an art form in itself. "Where are you going?" "Out." What parent hasn't been enlightened with some variation of the following? Notes left from their very own: "I'm out; love, me." "See you later; I love you." "Somebody called." or just a number unembroidered with any superfluous data like "555-6173" left on the message pad. Are you suppose to do what with that one? And that's when they are being responsible citizens and are telling you where, with whom, when, why and how! That's not all the rest of the time. It's the "Teenage Specific Syndrome". They are masters of the art of being vague. And usually they'll tell you only what they think you want to hear anyway. Most of what follows is from younger kids.

"Mrs. X is the library aide for the school. She gets her kicks making people leave the library when they talk. Mrs. X also is a pompus, rude, fat, obnoxious, overspoken, stupid, weird, disgusting, grose, disgustingly grose, four eyed, and all around real jerk. As you can tell I don't really like her. . ."

"School is one of the worst places in the world. You meet enemies who are allways saying bad things to you at school. If you finally fight your enemies, someone is always ready to stick up for them whether they lose or not. 99.9% of the teachers at school are real jerks. Only once in a while do you find a really good teacher. The friends you do make are always being put down, and if you don't put them down, people will look at you and think you're strange. Someone puts you down and calls you stupid. Then when you get strait A's they call you a dexter. In school you feal pressured to do things that you would not ordinarily do. It seems kind of strange almost, when someone's talking about how drunk or high they got, and you don't know what it feels like."

"happy home Resipie
(2) cups of tenderness
(1) cup of loyalty
(12) cups of love
(8) cups of friendship
(6) cups of thoughtfulness
Mix love through Friendship
Beat thoughtfulness good with tenderness
Sprinkel a pinch of faith with shreded hope
Serve with a littel loyalty"

From a letter writing exercise to Dear Abby:
"Dear Abie, I have a problem in one of my classes. That is my fifth period class. My teachers name is Mr. X. He gives too much homework even on the weekends and holidays. I would like to know how to control him. P.S. Don't tell him I said this. Yours truly,"

"Dear Abby, We are very low on money right now. My dad is going to close his store he owns a oriental rug store. He has owned it for seven years and now has to close it. We are trying to find some work for him but haven't. I was wondering if you could give us some ideas. Sincerely yours,"

"Dear Abby, My father lives in Ohio and I live in California. I haven't seen him in two years. My mother won't allow us to go back and see him until he pays her back all the money he owes her. And he owes too much money to pay it all back. He also has to raise two other children too. All I want is to see my father again. What shall I do? signed, depressed."

"Dear Abby, I have a half sister who will be a year old this December. She is small for her age and very quiet. She also, at times tends to use her right side more than she does her left. She isn't walking or talking yet. And is just now beginning to crawl instead of dragging herself on her stomach. The thing I would like to know is if there might be something wrong with her because I once heard that quiet babies sometimes tend to have something wrong. Is there a chance she just might be a slow developer, and how can I get my father and stepmother to listen to me? signed, Concerned."

"Dear Abby, I borrowed my mom's car and I had an accident. The car has a great big dent in the front, right fender. My mom is on vacation and won't be home for three weeks. I don't have the money to fix the fender. My mom doesn't know I even borrowed the car and it's brand new. What should I do? Sincerely, A Wreck." (When mommie-dearest came home and saw the damage, she cut huge patches out of the boy's well-care-for and stylish hair. He was ridiculed at school on Monday and Tuesday. He returned with a buzzed, short-cropped haircut on Wednesday.)

"Dear Abby, During the 5th grade I stole something very expensive. Now, when something is missing they come straight to me, even though I didn't do it. When they find what they lost they don't apologise. What should I do? Sincerely,"

"Dear Abby, I have a little puppy at home that is always barking at night. I can't get him to be quiet at night. My dad said if he doesn't shut up he is going to give him away. What should I do? singed, sad (X'd out) Concerned"

"Dear Abby, I have a difficult problem. Last week I

had to go to town to pick up an important bike part, and I saw my dad with another woman in a restaurant through the window. So I watched them and finally they got up and my dad kissed this woman. My confusion is this: 1. Should I tell my mother? 2. Confront my dad with what I saw? 3. Just leave things alone, and hope she was a friend. Signed, Confused"

"Some of these kids are smart in school, dumb in life." (a student)

"I'm going to my cousin Lisa's bas-mitzvah. I have a funny feeling that hers is going to be better than mine."

"I don't think that I could get a girl with all of those qualities, with my not so hot looks. . . .People always make fun of my nose."

"I didn't get to go to Hawaii for two weeks because I had been so smart assy."

'For Christmas I want a bench press. I have fast metabolism so I don't gain much. I want to be stronger than I am now. If I weight lift I might gain weight."

"In my life I've had a lot of sicknesses. For one thing, I'm a very allegic person."

'We went to a reception at Marsha's mother's house, such a rich neighborhood."

"I hate my little brother. If I'm vacuuming he just stands there; if I'm making my bed, he sits on it; when I'm baby-sitting he always stays out with his friends; he's always getting me into trouble."

"I think that my New Years resolution will be not to fight with my brother. I sure hope that his resolution will be not to fight with me."

"How come I seem to have a million problems and worries in my head?"

'How come it seems everybody has it easy and I have it so difficult? Everybody gets what he wants, and I don't."

"I just can't believe how much money parents spend on their kids. They just spoil them and buy them everything the kids ask for. Actually, I think that's sad because when the kid grows up he/she won't know how to spend their money right. I have to buy most of my clothes; sometimes my mom helps me out, but still, I know how to save and spend on the right things. Yes, I'm jealous because some kids have every-thing and I don't. But, I can't do anything about it, because we're not millionaires." (This is the student who "borrowed" her mother's diamond and pearl ring which she lost. She hasn't told her mother about that yet.)

"it was one of those days; i got up late and my brother and sister ate all the doughnuts. Then i missed my bus and my mom made me walk. i missed my first class and got de-tention. Then i had a test in third period that i didn't know about. After school when i was going to detention, i saw my best friend with my boyfriend. No one could have a worse day than this."

"Mondays are so depressing and boring. It's so far away from Friday."

"Male menopause means mid-life crises which means my old man was screwed up in the brain. Male menopause usually happens when the male reaches 40 to 50.

My dad left 1 year ago. During that time my dad came down every weekend to see me and my sister.

I am 14 and my sister is 17. My mom and dad were getting a divorce but my dad came to his senses so they didn't. My dad came down one day because he was going to stay with us for a few days and he ended up moving in in March.

My mom and dad are working on a reconsilliation. My mom and dad were married for 21 years before they were sepearated. It is not good to leave your family because it affects a lot of people that care about that person who leaves. . . .I have learned a lot from this experience."

"Last weekend I went to my dad's. It was really fun. I hadn't seen my dad for about a month."

"On Wednesday my mother slapped me across the face. My face is bruised where she slapped me. She dug her fingernails in then and drew blood. I hope that it doesn't leave a scar."

"My mother favors Lisa, my 11 year old, bratty sister. I hate her, too."

'Things I can't stand in this world are drugs, hippies, and homos."

"I hate my mother. She is so two-faced. One minute we'll be laughing and goofing around; and the next half-second, she'll be a grouch. I can't stand it. Out of all the moms in the world — Why me? I'm so sick of her; I really hate her guts. She always tells me stuff and then never does what she said she would."

"I hate it here. I feel like running away from home. I'm so sick of their nagging me. I don't think I'll be able to live here until I'm eighteen. Either I'll kill her or she will kill me or I'll kill myself."

"We went all over. It was so much fun. We went to a mall, to the beach, and then the harbor. We ate at Casa Maria and we walked around the marina. I got a pair of Gloria Vanderbilt black denim jeans. I also got a pair of wierd sweats and a pair of black pumps. Then I got a Thirty-one Flavors ice cream cake, a rose, and balloons. My little sister gave me some jellybellies. After that we went to Round Table Pizza, then the Arcade. I am going to get a lot more stuff later. I would have gotten more stuff, but my mom saved two hundred and fifty dollars, but she made an error in her checkbook. We ended up with thirty-two dollars."

"I hate my mom's boyfriend. He practically beats us to death. He always hits us for nothing. He owns a sailboat and him and my mom sleep on it a lot and we stay at home all night by ourselves. I wish I could live with my dad; I love him so much."

"Friday, I got in a fight with my mom so I walked to school. When I was halfway to school, my mom tried to pick me up and I said, 'If you touch me, I'll scream.' So she grabbed me and I started to scream. She got pissed so I said, 'I hate you' and I kept saying that. Then she drove me to school and she wanted me to talk to Mr. Adler (the vice principal). I broke loose from her and I started screaming, 'I hate you'. So I ditched school. Then after school I came back and caught the bus. I went to my friend's house till five. She was going to sneak me to spend the night; but she had company, so she couldn't. I went home and talked it out with my mom. . . .I told her, 'I ditched'; she was kinda mad, but she wrote a note and said, 'if there's any problems to call her'."

"I think I like Eric, but I don't really know. There's one thing that stands in the way of my liking him, because he's black."

"Back to school today, and everyone has new clothing on. Me and Vicky didn't get hardly anything."

"I hate Georgina Davis; she's such a scum; Joe is going with her; he doesn't like her; I can tell why. I heard she's really scared of me. I also heard she fucked Brian Marks. Let me tell you about my plan to get Georgian to break up with Joe. The reason for this is that I can be mean to Georgina, and my friend Heidi can get together with Joe. You see, there's something in it for both of us. Tonight we don't have Bible study; it's been changed to Wednesday."

"I finally got to walk home from school. You see, I've been grounded for three years."

"I wish I had a gun for I could shoot all the KKK people and they won't bother my friend know more. But the imigration would still bother him. Then I would have to shoot all of them too. I would like to be in a war. Like world war 3. But I don't want to get killed. Because it wouldn't be fun getting killed."

'My dad was so mad he threatened to send me to a Christian school."

"I learned about sportsmanship in Puerta Vallarta. Those guys can't really play worth shit, but they don't care. They have such a good time playing and being with one another; and that's what's important."

'We were watching *Pennies From Heaven* on T.V. Steve Martin started swearing. And my dad turned the channel."

"My dad doesn't allow me to read those sorts of books, but I read them anyway."

"I would like to be Jacklyn Smith (a TV actress on *Charlie's Angels*) because she is a very pretty person and doesn't seem like she has any problems.

If I was her on Monday's I would go to the modeling studio to take a couple pictures for the magazines. On Tuesday through Thursday I would be filming my movies and T.V. shows. Friday I would go to the beach, go shopping or ride horses. On Saturday I would eather play tennis or go somewhere fun. That night I would go to a party, come home and sleep in till about 10:30 a.m. I would go to church and after church I'd have my hair, nails, face, and then teeth done. I will now be ready to go home relax and go back to work on Monday. If it was the winter I would probably take off about 3 weeks and go to Mammoth with a couple of friends. Then take my limo to the lodge. Rent a suite and let my bodyguards ski too while I pay. I would like to be her because she doesn't seem to have any problems."

"I'm dreaming about one now. But I half to write this Day Dream Stuff! I hope I will get together with this chick But I don't know If she likes me. I would ask her but that takes an Insaine man, or more Balls, then Brains, to do that!"

'Every month I would fly my airplane to town and get drunk with my dreamgirl."

"Then I came across this dirty magazine. It was full of rad looken' nude chicks. I dreamt I was with these girls in the picture. I have always wanted to do that."

"After the concert I go back stage. I get a million dollars and lots of drugs. I always use drugs so do most disco people. It sure is great to be a star."

"I had fun on Monday. I got in a fight with Lori and she chickened out, so I never had a chance to really beat her up."

"Tonight I have Bible study. I can't wait. Judy P. is coming to pick me up. She is one of the greatest people to be with when you're drunk. . . .I was just talking to Janie about sucking on a guys dick or cock or whatever. She thinks it's gross but me and Suzy don't. I had fun last night. Judy and I went to Bible study and after we took our booze, car, and Jim down the hill and both of us gave him head. But I think Judy is kind of chicken." (Student name and telephone number withheld by parent request and the vice squad.)

"I can hardly wait till I'm eighteen. Because when I'm eighteen I don't have to ask my mom if I can go to any mad parties. And also so I can stay at my coaches house overnight (she's twenty-three). She's not like an ordinary twenty-three year old. Most people that age won't give us kids any booze. She will like one night after we lost our all star game, she took about three of us to a restaurant. All of her bitchen friends went. They ordered three pitchers of beer and enough glasses for all of us." Later, at the coach's house, "At about 4:30 she made strawberry margaritas. When she was pouring the phone rang. . .she went to answer it. Me and Liz guzzled all five tall margaritas. Then she made a new batch so we all drank two more. After the margaritas we went to Stephie's house. Her mom is really cool and lets us drink too. All me and Liz had was a beer."

Later, the coach went down and bought beer and toilet paper. "She said I had had enough to drink. So we snuck two more beers each and went out to the car. . .me and Liz were wasted. They took us inside. . . .Then we went toilet papering. When the people heard us, they ran and dragged me and Liz into the car. (We don't remember, but this is what they told us) We both passed out in the car. We woke up and we were sick as dogs. I could barely walk."

"I day dream all kinds of things. I usually day dream in class, Because theres nothing else to do. I like to day dream when i'm borred."

"Last weekend was really boaring. My parents were out partying; I had no fun at all."

"My dad is on the Bored of Education."

Do you remember the VP who was co-habitating with the teacher, and the teacher was transferred to another school and they were accused of immoral activities because they lived together? Good grief. Whose house needs a little tidying up now? If the VP and the teacher were being accused of potentially corrupting youth, after some of these autobiographical true confessions, it seems that it's too late for that. It must have happened already in the households of the pious ladies of the PTA.

133

I wonder who the PTA ladies would have thought it more appropriate for the VP and the teacher to live with rather than with one another if that was their choice? I believe that vows of poverty, chastity, and obedience are taken for a profession other than public school teaching.

Perhaps the ladies need to reconsider how they view members of the opposite sex. Maybe that's not such a bad fit after all; I think that sex is here to stay, no matter how the ladies of the PTA may try to deny that.

The VP's legitimate mate (in the sight of God as well as in the civil sense) had taken off over the hill with a new dalliance. The VP had been left with two teenage children to raise alone. Now is a single person better able to cope with the day to day challenges of raising a family, or is there a better balance if there is one of each gender in a household? And is that another reason why God has created both so that they can work together in greater harmony with one another? What do you think those PTA ladies could have thought was so bad about what was being done in that dwelling place to warrant their censure? My, my, those ladies certainly have active and fertile little minds, haven't they? Isn't it interesting that the teacher and the VP, even though assigned to different schools, are still living together? The outraged ladies of the PTA and the spineless district administration have changed only the appearance and not the substance of anything after all.

If the PTA ladies were concerned that the VP and the teacher weren't going to be adequate role models for their children, it must be said at last, it's hard for any sensible adult to be a role model these days. Obviously, the PTA ladies haven't done so well for all of their presumed uprightness, either.

If the schools expel all of the pupils who have already been corrupted in order to satisfy the high standards of the PTA ladies, there may not be any need for schools at all. And that would give the ladies one less important thing to do in their useful and busy lives.

When I was a boy, there was a saying that had the gist, it went something like, the general idea was, it went as I recall, "Let he who is without sin among you, cast the first stone." And there was another expression that I remember and found particularly appealing, too. It was, "live and let

134

live." I've got another slogan: "Down with the moral uplift society."

There is a postscript to this saga, a happy ending at last and love conquers all. The VP and the teacher have announced their intention to become honorable members of the community and make their dreadfully illicit arrangement legal in the eyes of the law and God and of the ladies of the PTA just as soon as a divorce is final. And everyone wishes them well; they are both really nice people. Perhaps the ladies of the PTA might better stay home and learn to prepare nutritious meals for their families. Some of them have been zero-basing an essential obligation of being a parent. In Army terms, "they ought to have their asses kicked."

What are people doing with their precious time saved from being concerned with their diets? What could be more important than staying healthy?

When I was a boy there was a limerick which went: 'In days of old when knights were bold and dames were not particular, they lined them up against the wall and screwed them perpendicular."

Now, before anyone gets his moral outrage up, let's take a little trip back to yesteryear, the good old days of *my* youth, not yours; because mine is *the* standard of the world, and yours isn't to me. I only remember what I want to about my own youth anyway, and that *very* selectively, when knights were bold and dames were not only particular but pure, when music wasn't decadent and too loud, a time when the world wasn't going to pot. They just drank too much, instead. (You got it. Now, what was that technique called again? Remember in education everything has to be repeated three times).

For as long as I can remember, there was always a class slut. Peg was called Pig behind her back. She was available to the reigning athletic hero if he had a) a car, or b) another place, or c) the nerve to ask nicely. She was the student body. Her clothing often looked as if it had been sent out from Frederick's in a plain wrapper. She wore some strange combinations devised by a mind that was clearly preoccupied with something other than fashion (or academics, either). She was into attraction instead. Everyone recognized where she was coming from or going

135

to and there were no hassles. Only years later did she go legit and join the Birch Society when her morals spread to politics as well.

Today she would wear plastic dangle earrings to match her eyeshadow, snap her gum just as ferociously as her predecessor, not walk, but flounce into classes, and talk about almost everything as fully this and fully that. She's Cindi with the huge circles over the i's. It won't take too many years before she has huge circles under her eyes as well. And we don't have to change the names to protect the innocent, either.

Do the kids quail over her any more than in the old days? Not at all. They'll only get offended if she oversteps her role and tries to push her weight around. If she calls someone she perceives as a wimp, a dexter, or a faggot, then the remark will be, "but consider the source."

Luv ya, Susi

"She has diseases penicillin's afraid to touch." (a student)

"Why don't we have a sex education class in junior high?" "I think you may have one in high school." "It's too late by then." (a student and teacher exchange)

"My girlfriend and I went out for dinner last night to celebrate." The teacher asked, "What was the special occasion?" "The last day of her period."

"Is gonorrhea the future tense of to have gone awry?" (a teacher)

And what other values have these same parents helped instill in their very own?

"Your new retainer! May I try it on?" (a student)

Another writing assignment, a composite: If you could have three wishes. . .anything in the world? "For my first wish I would like. . .two tons of the purest gold; all of the money in the world; a $500,000 shopping spree in New York; $100 a day, every day of my life; a lot of money; $100 billion trillion dollars; I'd like to be rich, rich, rich and filthy rich; to have my own Nieman-Marcus; a $1,000 a week allowance; one million dollars in cash; some beachfront property in New Zealand, to stop drinking hard liquor and beer, so I'd like myself a lot better; the aging process to stop at 21; to never get old and die; my parents to stop smoking; no more wars and no more hunger; a new math teacher; to live on an island all by myself where it's peaceful; my dog brought back to life; meet my favorite television star; to be adopted by my stepdad; to have a father; everyone to be happy; to have a happier family; to have God come alive on earth; to have the bus not be so crowded in the morning; to create history; to have all my enemies as my slaves; to be the ruler of the world."

Even if you make an allowance for California as being the land of fruits and nuts, and loony tunes, you still have to acknowledge that it (with New York) sets styles and trends. And it's said that those will be standard fare in every little hamlet nationwide within six months. Do I feel sorry for you out there.

Ah, those carefree years! The kids who made those statements are out there. Some just like them may be in your class next hour or next year. Some of their lives are really depressing. This is just a sampling; examples could have gone on and on. But why dwell on the obvious problem that some kids come to class with their attention *primarily* on something other than school or learning at all. There seem to be so many minor diversions from the primary job of learning. Faulty nutrition, lack of rest or exercise, daily life in these comfortable suburban households take their toll in academic slouch and student misbehavior. No matter what, even though their attention wanders obviously, you must be patient and forgiving parents as teachers, often better than those other ones at home.

And with a sub there, these kids often have a day that's not as comfortable as an ordinary one with the real teacher. If even a single class hour falls apart, for some of these kids with real problems, that's a high percentage of chaos in a life which often has little order outside of school.

To Wrap Up Some Loose Ends; The Summing Up; In Summary:

I said earlier that I couldn't think of a way to tell whether a kid was star-fucking you. Perhaps there is a way. The kid you'll never have in class because he's not capable of passing your subject, the ones you would meet on the street when you're only a sub and they greet you as an old friend, the kid who willingly and voluntarily wants to spend some time with you before, during, and after school and chat with you, is probably not star-fucking you.

Remember the teacher and her husband who looked like Barbie and Ken dolls? She was too thin (but not rich enough for her taste, I'm sure; what wife ever is?), and who was wearing all of those layers of underwear to keep herself warm probably because she had no fat to make her body comfortable? She has been out of school a lot recently. Reportedly she's not feeling too well for some reason.

When I was a boy, we were instructed that to become an adult you had to develop a sense of independence, a concern for others, an ability to do the right thing in case of emergency, be competent and self-sufficient and a lot of other things, but the goal was to become adult. You were to hone your body, mind, and spirit. A woman who obviously spends too much time concerned only with the way she looks becomes pathetic, absurd, and somewhat scary, as obviously her priorities are a bit misguided. There's an enormous difference between doing what you can with the little bit you have to work with versus an all consuming narcissism. Mirror, mirror on the wall? Beauty is a lot more complicated than how you look.

"Who are you today?" Try, "I forgot" and see what happens. That'll confuse them.

In relation to creative phraseology, would anyone ever expect a pseudo-scatalogical emphasis for the subtitle of a substitute handbook? Believe me, it took a certain amount of genius to work that one out, but I admit to that only reluctantly and somewhat humbly. Sometimes you need to create your own verbal Potemkin Village. It's verbal sleight of hand: Now you hear it; now you don't. Now it's here and then it isn't. Pouf!

The teenage years are very sexual; they're the time to define and then refine yourself. Sex, excessively then, is a continuing theme in thought and deed throughout these years and in these *Confessions*, as it is an integral part of the reality of a school. Students have enormous and rapid physical changes; they're often on an emotional roller-coaster. It's a time to begin to learn the little reality that average is a lot lower than you ever thought it was. And while they have to learn the boundaries of acceptable behavior, they are also having to learn not to be children and childish anymore, but are being expected to understand that the reason for devoting all of those years to learning something was to prepare them to function as a responsible adult in a real world. It's a very confusing time. The society was willing to invest its hard-earned money in their future only if it thought that it was getting its money's worth. And in at least a million cases each year, it wasn't.

Try this recipe for chocolate pudding (instead of the one on page 123):

Chocolate Pudding

3 T cornstarch
1/2 cup sugar
3 T cocoa
Mix with a half cup of milk to a smooth paste; add 1-3/4 cup milk and stir over medium heat until thickened. Add 1-2 t. vanilla. Serves 6 (unless you have a teenage son).

That whole section on the Duchess of Windsor and Adolph Hitler began as something of a lark. In the beginning I was just playing around with some ideas; and then when I could add in some bonafide heavy in the sinister plot from ITT to round it out, it began to make more sense all the time. Beware of the Ides of ITT. They're now buying into financial services companies. Remember what J. P. Morgan said about those who control the availability of money? If you control the availability of money, you can control governments.

If you ever really want to get away from it all (I mean from real life itself for the great escape), stay at one of ITT's Sheraton Hotels. They're a bit impersonal, but you can indulge yourself; you can have it all and you can have it now, hermetically sealed, of course. It's an interesting and necessary experience for the whole family.

Even Hostess Twinkies aren't being singled out particularly as being worse for you than other types of fun foods. Actually, by my definition, they're either "shit food" in military parlance; (treacle is pretty close to fecal and offal is awful) or unfood. ITT isn't producing a billion of those things so that they can gather dust in a warehouse someplace. Someone's consuming what they're producing and I'm not one of them. That means that someone out there is getting double rations.

ITT is used as a symbol only of the impersonality within a system that concerns itself almost exclusively with the bottom line approach, rather than with a greater regard for some other values. ITT is made up of real fathers, uncles, mothers, and cousins who would protect you with their lives if you were one of their own. There seems to be a tendency toward an impersonality as a result of the size and enormous power that kind of all-pervading institution can wield, however.

And I'm not putting the Gay Rights' Movement down either. What someone chooses to do in the privacy of his own bedroom should be of no one else's concern. Can you imagine living in a society in which a freedom of choice would be denied? And someone would be watching over, able, and quite willing to tell you what to believe and how to conduct your personal activities? That's a little dictatorial and totalitarian, Big Brotheresque for my taste. I distrust people who either know it all or have easy answers for complex issues and circumstances. "Kill 'em all." (a student)

If there are 225,000,000 people in the U.S. today and 10% of those are gay if Kinsey statistics are still valid, that's 22,500,000 people by extrapolation. If we accept killing as a positive solution, that's a lot of funerals, flowers, lost technology, forgotten mathematical and chemical formulas, lessened insights, etc. It may seem positive to some perhaps but decidedly negative for a lot more. It may be time for a cost-benefit analysis.

As my wife put it, when our own boys were younger and feeling threatened and freaking out over the gay community, ."If you find yourself in a difficult situation that you don't want to be in, you always have the option of saying, No, and then do a fast fade."

However, what I do object to is that a grown man would be such a flamer (that's localeze for a flaming faggot, an overt and very feminine type), that he would be willing to expose himself to groups of pre-pubescent boys at a time in their lives when they don't need that; that he would be willing to paint his fingernails red and orange and make a spectacle of himself as a mockery of his gender, and generally take advantage of the position of surrogate teacher to promote his own personal ends. I think that's inexcusable.

I've inserted here and there some Army expressions and no wonder being drafted into this mans' army was something of a shock. We said almost as standard operating procedure at the dinner table, "Please pass the fucking butter." Even paper toilet-seat covers had a special name; they were "ass-gaskets". Bavarian winters were "as cold as a witch's tit". A woman who was generously endowed was "built like a brick shithouse". "Shit kickers" were western movies, an annoyance "pissed you off", "piss-poor" was bad quality, and "SOS" was served on toast. "Half-assed" was done badly, "haul-ass" was hurry up, "dragging-ass" meant you were tired. If you "fucked-up" and when "the shit hit the fan" or "your tit was in the wringer", you were in "deep-shit", "SOL", or "up a creek without a paddle" and you would be summoned to the orderly room via the 'bitch-box" to have your "ass chewed". It went on and on. It was all the lowest common denominator as my mother would have put it, primitive (and very anal).

However, it still doesn't make you more manly or a better fighter or really much of anything except a foul-mouth if you use those terms. It's all such unnecessary vulgarity and that perhaps ought to be reconsidered as an acceptable standard in the military and in the civilian sector as well. For shame, Christina Crawford, you've made a bad situation even worse. I think that some among us (and I'm included) have been suckered gradually into accepting more and more filth as an acceptable way of expressing ourselves. Perhaps the language is rich enough without it.

If anyone thinks he recognizes himself or sees an aspect of another teacher in the teacher profile section, especially, I'm really sorry for that. I tried to keep examples as vague as possible as composite types but with enough information to indicate that there was something wrong, potentially at least. Please don't feel embarrassed, betrayed, angry, or hurt by what has been said. Remember, I wasn't describing individuals, but types. All we can try to do is learn; and some lessons are often more painful than others. It's always hard to think that you are being interpreted by someone who doesn't really know you all that well, and that's true in this case as well.

Another major concern for me, personally, was the

potential reaction of students who might read the handbook and feel that the times we spent together were just manipulative sessions. Quite the contrary, the more relaxed they were with me, the more genuinely comfortable I felt being with them, too. I really enjoyed their company. They are nice kids.

My wife guards students' journals very carefully. All names were changed so that student identification would be virtually impossible.

If the PTA in your school is functioning, count your blessings. All too typically, after the taco salad has been served at the faculty pre-school luncheon, that organization folds up its tent and fades away into the sunset. The organized PTA is used symbolically anyway, as we're all parents and teachers in or out of a classroom as soon as we have children.

And Michelle? The last time I saw her she was like another person. One classmate was plaiting her hair in a complicated braid and she had become a person to like really rather than to be wary of.

Remember the boy who was describing the time factors in the movie, *"Star Wars"*? He is a highly imaginative and creative humanities type. And those unimaginative doltish clods who couldn't follow his reasoning process. . .?

The relatively big and brawny low-end boy had misbehaved in class; his parents had been called the night before about his behavioral transgressions and his lack of academic achievement as well. The father was an underling in the Group. In class the following day he made every attempt to disrupt class by trying to organize a general rebellion. But no other student chose to join him. After school he was to pick up a listing of uncompleted assignments from his teacher.

In the classroom, when he got there, was another of his own Group, younger, smaller, but brighter and more capable in many ways. His diet is more balanced as a starter; his father is reputedly the local chieftain of the Group and they maintain close ties with the old country and more old-fashioned ways.

The little one leaned back in his chair; his voice became imperious; and he said, "Hey, you. You misbehaving in this teacher's class?" The bigger boy, standing in front of him answered, "I got a detention." "You'd better not do that." with his voice lowered, the bigger one then lowered his head and avoided any eye contact and said quietly, "Yeah."

There are a lot of power plays in school; many you won't recognize because you're an adult and not a child. But they happen every day.

The worst one for me, I think, was the one with Scott and the Black kid. Both of them were really nice boys, but Scott at least was coming on with an approach I never had to reconsider. That kind of racial intolerance was not part of the standard passed on by the area of the country where I grew up and certainly not by my parent; and I thank her for that.

Actually our bigotry was programmed against unthinking, smug WASPS. We were expected to judge people on the standards they represented themselves and on their approaches with people they had contact with. Sometimes those criteria were a bit lofty in the face of the reality of what seemed possible (unless you were Godly), but you were expected to respect all people and treat them fairly and courteously.

If you have spent some time out of the country, it's difficult to feel all that superior about who you are when you have been disliked and distrusted or misjudged, not because of who you are individually, but who you are supposed to be as a stereotypical American. Love they neighbor is easier. Greener grows the grass on the other side of the river or the fence in many ways, but not in all ways as you probably know. And it's still a long road that has no turning.

And the next day, the big one came on like a lamb; the little one, like a lion. It's necessary then for the teacher to re-establish his authority as the boss of bosses.

Correct and grade this one at your leisure; it's especially difficult to understand the native tongue, to have been graduated from an institution of supposedly higher learning, teach all day, and then go home to your own family, their needs and expectations, dinner preparation, the day's mail (and required responses) and then face a hundred or so of these. Progress reports are due the day after tomorrow. But take your time!

Gerald, French
Period 1
Book Report
(teacher's name, misspelled)
English

:Book Report:

Tittle: The Cay
Auther: Theodore Taylor
Copy Rite: 1969 by Avon Books Inc.
The Plot: The plot was that a young boy named Phillip and his family were in a War time situation and the mother decieded to leave while they stil could. They left on a big ship and about 30 miles off shore they were hit by a torpedo. Everybody got on different life boats and phillip ended up with a very old collord man.
Main idea; The main idea was That Phillip and the collord man get stranded on a deserted island and phillip gets blined. Now they have to live there until sombody rescues them.
Opinion: My opinion of thebook was that it was great and i think everybody should reed it. It was a great adventure story:
Theme:

And then there's behavior. When the boy and girl sat across the work table from one another and exchanged first of all heavy breathing and then orgasmic moans and cries, "Just practicing", they exclaimed; and an older, more jaundiced type remarked, "You've both been self-inflicting too long, you're not even doing it right", you know then that times have changed considerably since you were a boy.

Here's another standard that I've reconsidered but have decided to stick to tradition after all. If someone puts his feet on a table and you find that offensive, just say, "Please don't do that; our floor isn't clean enough to eat from."

The principal told the teacher that to solve the problem of the boy farting in class on cue, that she was to follow school policy and first assign the boy fifteen minutes detention; the second time, call the parents; the third time, to send in a note to the office and they would hold him after school. Isn't that just like a principal? Before the teacher had finished this lengthy and well-thought-through-process, the whole class was farting on cue. And they're still doing it, and dropping their books on cue, and throwing paper balls on cue. That teacher needs to listen more selectively for good advice, not bad, and then act on that. That advice has got to be reasonable and appropriate for solving that particular problem or situation. You can't apply the same solution to every problem as the administration tries to do. Everything is different and that's nice because it gives life some zest and makes you feel good. And go out among those children and love them.

The kid who started it and who was in another teacher's early class (and he often came early to visit with for some reason), said to her, "Mrs. Smith, what would you do if I farted in class?" And she said, "Gee, Ned, I wouldn't do anything. It's not my problem; it's your stomach." He's probably never done that kind of behavior around that teacher anyway and probably never will. Incidentally, farted was the acceptable term in Shakespeare's day in Elizabethan England.

Remember the teacher who had said that she would laugh if a boy farted in class? Guess what just happened to her. This note was found on her desk: "Dear Mrs. X. We all hate you, you know. The reason is that we don't think you know very much."

The teacher who received this note was going to track down the culprit by matching the paper style; it had a distinctive red line down the margin. The writer's printing style was to be compared with examples from student work. There was a great emphasis on finding out *who* had done it. Not *why*?

What were various teacher's solutions to what to do about this situation? One teacher said, "They love doing the newspaper. I'd take that away from them." Another said, "I'd give them seatwork for the rest of the year." Another said, "May I use that as an example for one of my classes, the whole idea of cruelty to one another." (Even though she was asked not to use it, she still did it anyway. So much for being able to trust your colleagues.) Another said, "Don't do anything until you know exactly what you want to do." Only the last suggestion was even sane. Even though this may have been the last straw for a teacher whose life has more compications than just school, even then, don't let your ego dictate a bad solution to the problem. The note came from a single student presuming to act for them all, but even that was left unsigned.

Suggestion to solve or at least reduce the anxiety of such a situation: Give the students a two to three week scatter-shot orientation of everything you've always wanted them to know about your topic and then call each student up to your desk, chat with each individually, and in the course of the conversation ask each: 1) what he wants to get out of the class, 2) how best that can be achieved, and 3) what could be done to improve the atmosphere of the class? Have each then essentially do a contract with you; and they map out a study program for themselves, the things that they want to know. And hopefully you won't get any more notes like that one. It's worth a try anyway; you know that those other options are ridiculous. Don't question anyone about who wrote the note; who did it is irrelevant. The teacher only needs to correct a bad situation in that class. To laugh would not have been an adult reaction; it would have been infantile behavior. Examples like that would be transmitted to students in many ways; and if a teacher has classes of the top range, they can't respect him.

Later, she even got a poison-pen note from a parent which addressed her as, "Dear Mrs. Ane," French slang which meant that the teacher was regarded as an ass. That wasn't a very adult approach on the parent's part and a terrible example for the child.

To say that you don't like a food that you later admit you've never tasted is infantile also. Life needs some variety so don't limit yourself to narrow constrictions but, instead, expand and grow.

It's curious that all of this should happen to one of the best organized teachers, personally dedicated, inspired (she has some really exciting and stimulating lessons), one most willing to help her students or a fellow teacher. It's not very just.

Remember the teacher who advised having the kid "removed" from class (that's a pretty pretentious way to say kicked out)? She has begun to have more frequent contact with some members of the faculty; at home she has started to share the necessary chores of living that are simply a part of life itself (as they say in Mexico, "El trabajo es·la vida" or work is life and that can be reversed as well). Babies are not an abstraction; they mewl and puke in their mother's arms. Life is like that. She wants to learn how to make bread because she thinks that it would taste better; and she's right there, too. She is no longer hiding behind the Miss Dove role but is willing to let others see what a nice, human, human being she is. She has also become the friend of someone I'm very fond of.

Last but not least, believe me, as they used to say when I was a boy, whatever happened to the teacher who said that she wouldn't do anything, and that that behavior would go away only when it wasn't rewarded in any way? That was the very same lady who had students who came to be with her as frequently as possible (and everyone I know feels the same way). That's a sneaky way of dedicating a book to the women you love, isn't it? Not to my wife, Elizabeth, but to my real wife, Betty. Many thanks.

How many wives have ever had the gall to serve cheese souffle for dinner two nights running, not only because it's asparagus season, but because she knows that that is one of her husband's very favorite food combinations, with cheese sauce over all, a French roll with garlic butter, and salad, and milk, and some white wine and some excellent Chinese tea to follow (the country black kind with the stems left in and from the block) Pu Erh Beeng Cha it's called phonetically. Try it; I can recommend it highly. It's our favorite. Now that kind of dinner is my idea of fun food and heaven.

And thanks to our elder son, Max, who did the inspired line drawings for the handbook. I wish I were that talented.

The weathervane that was so unusual was actually made by a student in a woodshop class out of expensive laminated woods. The craftmanship was beautiful; you just had to go farther around the world to get to the position indicated than is ordinary. The traditional verbal order is not the physical order.

I hope that the handbook has been helpful. It could prove to be only the beginning, however, in trying to solve, at least partially, the substitute problem. So here's an invitation I hope you'll accept. It's not exactly like seeing your name in lights, but it's better to have it in print perhaps rather than not at all. I suppose for any teacher, the best is to be remembered kindly by your ex-students. Join the Share Your Success League. Share with the rest of us approaches that have really worked for you. Please be as specific as possible: what sort of group it has worked with, their age range, subject area; etc. Let's try to teach ourselves some new tricks.

I didn't really expect it to happen, but it did. Earlier it was, "Oh, good, you're here. Now we're not going to have the test." or, "Oh, good, you're here. I'm so glad Mr. Kent isn't here." Now get this one, "Oh boy, my favorite substitute." That felt pretty good, I think. Have a nice day, a really nice day.

149

I purposely didn't include a table of contents at the beginning of the handbook because I wanted you to have to read the total without being able to anticipate anything or skip ahead. It's hard to have ever been a teacher; you wish you could manipulate them all, but there's always that necessary exception to every rule (for you and for the culture, too).

The following is then a topical outline by page reference:

French got transferred back to where he
belonged, the class cheered to be rid of him.
But the class that got him instead, cheered
and was disruptive for the rest of the hour,
and was glad to have him back.

MOZART   GERALD, FRENCH   SHAKESPEARE